CRIMES IN
HOT COUNTRIES

FAIR SLAUGHTER

By the same author

Stage Plays
    Cheek
    No One Was Saved
    Alpha Alpha
    Edward, The Final Days
    Stripwell
    Claw
    The Love of a Good Man
    That Good Between Us
    The Hang of the Gaol
    The Loud Boy's Life
    No End of Blame
    Victory
    Downchild
    Birth on a Hard Shoulder
    A Passion in Six Days
    The Castle

T.V. Plays
    Cows
    Mutinies
    Prowling Offensive
    Conrod
    Heroes of Labour
    Russia
    All Bleeding
    Heaven
    Pity in History

Radio Plays
    *One Afternoon on the 63rd Level of the North Face
        of the Pyramid of Cheops the Great*
    Henry V in Two Parts
    Herman with Millie and Mick
    Scenes From an Execution

PLAYSCRIPT 107

CRIMES IN HOT COUNTRIES

FAIR SLAUGHTER

Howard Barker

JOHN CALDER · LONDON
RIVERRUN PRESS · NEW YORK

First published in Great Britain, 1984, by
John Calder (Publishers) Limited
18 Brewer Street, London W1R 4AS

and in the United States of America, 1984, by
Riverrun Press Inc
175 Fifth Avenue
New York, NY 10010

Fair Slaughter was originally published in 1978 by
John Calder (Publishers) Limited

All performing rights in these plays are strictly reserved and
applications for performance should be made to:

Judy Daish Associates Limited
83 Eastbourne Mews, London W2 6LQ

No performance of these plays may be given unless a licence has
been obtained prior to rehearsal.

British Library Cataloguing in Publication Data
Barker, Howard
   Crimes in hot countries; with Fair slaughter.
   I. Title   II. Barker, Howard. Fair slaughter
   822'.914   PR6052.A6485

ISBN 0 7145 4046 3

SUBSIDISED BY THE
Arts Council
OF GREAT BRITAIN

Library of Congress Catalogue Card Number: 84-71273

Typeset 9/10 pt Press Roman by Gilbert Composing Services,
   Leighton Buzzard, Bedfordshire.
Printed in Great Britain by Hillman Printers (Frome) Limited, Frome, Somerset.

CONTENTS

Crimes in
Hot Countries

Crimes in Hot Countries was commissioned by the RSC in 1978. It received its first performance as a rehearsed reading at the Almeida Theatre on 21 November 1982, with the following cast:

PORCELAIN	Toby Salaman
HACKER	Roger Sloman
STRUGGLE	Diane Fletcher
KNOTTING	Sian Thomas
TRELLIS	Veronica Roberts
TOPLIS	Michael Pennington
PAIN	Clive Merrison
ERICA	Jill Baker
ISTED	David Cardy
DOWNCHILD	Philip Barnes
DITCH	Michael Shevelow
MUSIC	Brian Hall
TALLBOY	Graham Lines
OLD	Arthur Whybrow
YOUNG	Paul Wilce
SLIPPER	David Lyon
CASHIN	Richard Addison

Directed by Ian McDiarmid

Its first full production was at the Theatre Underground, Essex University on 15 March 1983, with the following cast:

PORCELAIN	Ian Amos
HACKER	Rick Parker
STRUGGLE	Cheryl Gucwa
KNOTTING	Sara Green
TRELLIS	Alice Grant
TOPLIS	David Hallowes
PAIN	Ian Barnes
ERICA	Penny McHale
ISTED	Ron Levi
DOWNCHILD	James Holloway
DITCH	Mike Leach
MUSIC	Mike Bailey
TALLBOY	Colin Devine
OLD	Charlie Langdon-Mead
YOUNG	Andy Papadopoulos
CASHIN	Ian Amos
SLIPPER	John McVerry

Directed by Charles Lamb

ACT ONE

Scene One

The coast of a hot country. A MAN *staggers on stage bearing a massive bag. He drops it, falls to his knees, sobs violently. A* SECOND MAN *enters, carrying a very small bag. He watches the first.*

HACKER.   Compare my bag.
PORCELAIN.   Shuddup.
HACKER.   Look at my bag.
PORCELAIN.   No!
HACKER.   Go on. Compare it with yours.
PORCELAIN.   I have been staring at your bag for three solid weeks. I hate your bag!
HACKER.   It is a small bag, you see. It is a bag for happiness. Your bag has your whole life in it. You will never be happy while you have that bag.
PORCELAIN.   Please, you can see I'm crying. May I just cry on my own?
HACKER.   You have been crying since we left Tilbury.
PORCELAIN.   Well, can I just get on with it?
HACKER.   I tell you son, your suicide is in that bag. I have brought nothing with me, have I? All I want I shall find here. Every time you open that bag your eyes will fill with tears . . .
PORCELAIN.   All right, Thank you.
HACKER.   I'm helping you.
PORCELAIN.   You are not helping me.
HACKER.   He says I'm not helping him. (THREE WOMEN *enter, carrying bags*) I am helping him. *(They stare about them)* Very hot, isn't it? I was expecting heat but this is sheer extravagance. Still, I will adapt. I'm nothing if not an adaptor. I am going to like this place.
STRUGGLE.   I fail to see how any intelligent human being could be so rash as to make a forecast of that sort. It is barely five minutes since we stepped off the boat. Look, my little shoes are curling up!
HACKER.   I am going to like it because I want to like it. I will leave my bones here, Mrs Struggle. I shall not be dragging home, wrinkled as a peanut shell, to gob my final phlegm into a Bournemouth tea cup. Look, I kiss the soil! *(He kneels)* .
STRUGGLE.   Soil, he calls it . . .
HACKER.   I am no geologist. *(He kisses the ground)* Anybody got a glass of water?
STRUGGLE.   This dust would not support the plaster cast of a cactus.

A ship's hooter is heard. TRELLIS *suddenly bursts out weeping.*

HACKER. Mr Porcelain, look what you have started! Nothing is more catching than wet eyes.

STRUGGLE (*going to* TRELLIS). She had formed an attachment to the second officer.

HACKER. Yes, well, that is the way of women, isn't it?

KNOTTING. She will never make a proper bint, will she? Sandra? I despair.

STRUGGLE. Jane.

KNOTTING. Will she? She falls for every hairy arse that can splutter out a compliment.

STRUGGLE. You have lovely tits but I wish you would keep your ideas to yourself.

KNOTTING. I'm sorry, but I am a professional.

STRUGGLE. All right, be professional but keep your mouth shut. Sandra was never on a ship before. Were you darling? Never been afloat?

PORCELAIN (*climbing to his feet*). I shan't cry again.

HACKER. Don't commit yourself.

PORCELAIN. No. I have made up my mind.

HACKER. Mr Porcelain, you have untapped reserves of confidence.

PORCELAIN. Six months is not long, after all.

HACKER. The blink of an eyelid.

PORCELAIN. I shall be fully occupied with my report.

HACKER. You see, he conquers pain! I like you, Mr Porcelain. Even after three weeks in his cabin, I can say in all honesty, here is a man who can surprise me. I like that. What are you doing?

PORCELAIN. Throwing away my handkerchief.

A MAN *enters, rolling billiard balls up and down his arms.*

KNOTTING. Oh, blimey, look who's here . . .

They watch as TOPLIS *works his way across the stage. He completes his performance with a juggle that fails. The balls drop to the ground.*

TOPLIS. They have expanded in the sun. An infinitesimal increase in diameter and months of practice clatter to the floor . . . (*He begins to pick them up*)

HACKER. There is a saying among entertainers, I believe. Only a cold belly plays to hot soldiers.

TOPLIS. I like hot soldiers. It is hot soldiers I have come to play to.

STRUGGLE. Why has nobody arrived to pick us up?

TOPLIS. Mrs Struggle cannot wait to open shop! Ten minutes on dry land and she expects a queue! Give them time, Mrs Struggle. You will have their wages yet.

KNOTTING. You ungrateful bugger.

TOPLIS. This desert wind is very slow. Your perfumes have not yet drifted into camp . . .

KNOTTING. You didn't come 'alf as sarcastic up be'ind the lifeboats, Toplis.

STRUGGLE. Jane . . .

KNOTTING. 'e was all complimentary, then. The Bay of Malta 'eld no treasure like my 'ips. I quote.

STRUGGLE. Jane. The mouth. Less of it, please, lovely as it is.

TOPLIS. The definition of redundancy—flattering a prostitute. *(He begins juggling again)*

KNOTTING. Unless 'e wants to get under 'er clothes for free!

TOPLIS. I had no change.

HACKER. He had no change . . .

TOPLIS. I was obliged to spend the only currency I had. In profusion, I admit. But my vaults are easily replenished. Once you possess a word, it can be spent over and over again . . . *(He catches the balls)* Ole!

STRUGGLE. Toplis, this is a very small place.

PORCELAIN. Four thousand square miles, Mrs Struggle.

STRUGGLE. Four thousand, is it?

PORCELAIN. Of Oolitic limestone.

STRUGGLE. Thank you. So I recommend you keep a muzzle on your mouth. We will make friends here quicker than you do, and some of them clever with their fists and boots.

Sounds of a motorcycle. It wheels onto the stage, stops. A SOLDIER *climbs off, removes his goggles. He takes a paper from his breast pocket. They watch him.*

PAIN. I have a chit for china. *(They look blank)* Ex-London docks. *(They gawp)* Collect, deliver Government House. *(and gawp)* Were there no boxes from the boat? *(They shake their heads)* China—non—apparata—est. *(He scrawls on the chit, turns to go)*

PORCELAIN. Excuse me. I wonder if your chit says porcelain?

PAIN. That's right. China.

PORCELAIN. I'm Porcelain. Ronald Porcelain. Of Beckenham, Kent.

PAIN *(examining the chit casually)*. They forgot to tick the livestock box. Sign here, will you? *(He holds it out for* PORCELAIN *to sign)* It's typical of a modern army to issue forms of such rigorous specificity, but equally typical that the men employed to service them are barely literate. The common soldier is both the greatest obstacle to efficiency and the ultimate condition of it. He has to be driven to take a bath. He reads comics. His vocabulary consists of stale abuse. Yet these are the very factors that enable him to lay down his life by numbers. An army is a fallacy sustained by contradiction. *(He climbs on the motorcycle, turns to* PORCELAIN*)* Will you hold on very tight? I am inclined to be reckless. *(He pulls on his goggles.* PORCELAIN *gets on behind)*

STRUGGLE. What about the rest of us?

PAIN. Alas, I have no chits for you.

He starts the cycle, they drive away, watched into the distance by the others.

HACKER. A bob a bag.

STRUGGLE.   What?

HACKER.   A bob a bag.

STRUGGLE *(glaring at him)*.   We are fellow passengers!

HACKER.   Mrs, my fare took all my savings. I cannot be a gent as yet. (STRUGGLE *looks at the girls, back to* HACKER)

STRUGGLE.   Sixpence.

HACKER.   Ah, sixpence! How I would love to cart your bags for sixpence! Nothing would give me greater pleasure. Threepence? Sheer delight! Unfortunately my hands are tied my market forces.

STRUGGLE.   What market forces?

HACKER.   I am the only geezer here.

STRUGGLE.   Robber!

HACKER.   Now she abuses me.

KNOTTING.   Carry mine.

HACKER *(stepping forward)*.   Thank you. *(He looks at* TRELLIS) And you, Miss? (TRELLIS *shrugs*) Thank you. *(He bundles two under each arm)* Now I'm overloaded. Mrs Struggle, your bags will have to bear a surcharge.

STRUGGLE.   Mr Toplis, will you stand by and allow this?

KNOTTING.   'e's loving it.

STRUGGLE.   We are women in a strange country!

HACKER.   One and six.

STRUGGLE.   Are there no black men in this place?

HACKER.   One and tenpence.

STRUGGLE.   Never.

HACKER.   This way, ladies, follow the motorbike. *(He leads* KNOTTING *and* TRELLIS *away)*

STRUGGLE *(calling after him)*.   I came here to make money, not to give it away! *(She watches them disappear.* TOPLIS *throws up a ball, catches it on his forehead. He staggers about, juggling)* I don't care if my bowels fall through my crack, I'm not giving anything to him.

TOPLIS.   There speaks a woman of principle. *(She picks up her bags, starts to go out)* Rowena, we were fated to be left alone like this . . . *(He staggers forward, the ball on his forehead, unaware she has left)* We have not so much as kissed since Suez . . . *(He catches the ball on his neck now)* If I asked you to take your clothes off, I wonder if you would?

ERICA.   No. (TOPLIS *catches the balls. Pause)*

TOPLIS.   It's a funny thing, at moments of supreme concentration, I can detect the presence of a stranger. I can even tell if she is beautiful. *(He turns round. A* WOMAN *is standing behind him)*

ERICA.   I'm not.

TOPLIS.   All women are beautiful.

ERICA.   I see you go in for clichés.

TOPLIS.   When in desperation, say the first thing that comes in your head. It's a performer's maxim.

ERICA.   I have a version of the same thing. When in desperation, speak the truth.

TOPLIS.   Very good. I'm looking for the barracks.

ERICA. You undress. *(Pause)*

TOPLIS. The S.S. Orchid leaves a lot to be desired. If you travel tourist class . . .

ERICA. Go on.

TOPLIS. Where did you say the barracks was? *(Pause)*

ERICA. I carry a Webley 3.8.

TOPLIS. Scarcely the ideal weapon for a woman. Doesn't fit the handbag.

ERICA. I don't have a handbag.

TOPLIS. No, you don't . . .

Pause, then he kicks off his shoes, throws off his jacket, lets his trousers fall to the ground. He is naked. She looks at him.

ERICA. Not much of a wardrobe. Did someone steal your linen, or have you dispensed with it? Underwear is only fit for ripping, don't you find? Gets in the way of a proper masculine haste? *(Pause. She walks round him)* Gone all quiet now. Effect of nakedness. Kills chatter dead. *(Pause)* You have a scar on your arse. Big enough to lay a finger in.

TOPLIS. A bayonet.

ERICA. In your arse?

TOPLIS. I was running. Where else could he jab me? It is a little known fact that most soldiers' wounds are in their backs. *(She stops, looks him over)*

ERICA. If I see you again, I will think of you like this. Naked, arrogant, absurd. Your packet of treasures hanging apologetic. It's how all men should be seen . . .

She goes out. TOPLIS *scrambles into his clothes. Picks up the juggling balls, starts to go out. He stops, attempts a simple trick, but the balls fall to the floor. He picks them up, runs off.*

Scene Two

FOUR SOLDIERS *come in, three reading from identical books.*

ISTED. Gallia—est—omnis—divisa—in—partes—tres—

DOWNCHILD. quarum—unum—incolunt—Belgae—aliam—Aquitani—

DITCH. tertiam—qui—ipsorum—lingua—Celtae—

MUSIC. STOKES MORTAR ASSEMBLY!

ISTED. nostra—Galli—appellantur—

MUSIC. ONE!

DOWNCHILD. Hi—omnes—lingua—

MUSIC. BASE PLATE TO BASE PLATE LOCKING PIN!

DITCH. *(sitting cross-legged).* institutis—legibus—inter—se—differunt—

MUSIC. TWO!

ISTED. *(sitting to form a circle).* Gallos—ab—Aquitanis—Garumna—flumen—

MUSIC. BARREL SWIVEL ELEVATION RATCHET! LOCK!

DOWNCHILD. a—Belgis—Matrona—et—Sequana—dividit—

MUSIC. THREE!
ISTED. Eddie . . .
MUSIC. MARK VII DETONATOR RING!
ISTED. Eddie . . .
MUSIC. LOCK!
DOWNCHILD. I wish I understood Eddie . . .
MUSIC. RANGE! SEVEN HUNDRED YARDS!
DITCH. I understand Eddie.
MUSIC. FIRE!
DITCH. Eddie's in love . . .
MUSIC. FIRE! FIRE! FIRE! (*He collapses in helpless laughter.* PAIN *appears holding another copy of the book*)
PAIN. Sorry. Late again.
MUSIC. Private Pain, you bitch in a bunk-up, you.
PAIN. Sit in a semi-circle, shall we? (*He sits down. Only* MUSIC *remains standing*)
MUSIC. Oh, your puttee! Oh, your poxy puttee, slipping like a bint's bra at beano . . .
PAIN. I see you forget your book . . .
MUSIC. Shall I loop it for him?
PAIN. The Gallic Wars.
MUSIC. He shames me, the short-arsed shirk. I shall have to loop it. I cannot watch.
PAIN (*as he approaches*). No thanks.
MUSIC. No thanks? Have you clapped eyes on your boots?
DITCH. Eddie . . .
MUSIC. 'e 'as no socks!
PAIN. The cult of kit.
MUSIC. The what?
PAIN. The—cult—of—kit. (*Pause.* MUSIC *shakes his head*)
MUSIC. Fuck you, then.
PAIN. (*he wanders away, turns to listen*). Julius Caesar. Why do we remember Julius Caesar? (*They look blank*) Why do we bother with his books? (*Pause*) Stan? (DOWNCHILD *looks down*) Don? (ISTED *shakes his head*) Anyone?
MUSIC. Because 'e bunked off Cleopatra, Queen of Fuck.
PAIN. No, I don't think he did.
MUSIC. Because 'e 'ad the biggest rod in Roma!
PAIN. None of the chroniclers mentions it.
MUSIC. Well, 'e did, then! Dickus Monstrus was 'is nickname. Cockus Maximus! Fancy you not knowing that. (*Pause*)
PAIN. He was an innovatory tactician.
MUSIC. DON'T BE FILTHY!
DOWNCHILD. Eddie—
MUSIC. 'is filthy lingo is a permanent embarassment to me.
DOWNCHILD. Eddie—
MUSIC. Eddie what!

Pause. MUSIC *lies down, raises his legs in the air, opens them, closes them.*

PAIN. I'm going to fart . . . *(The others exchange amused glances)* A fart—to shoot my rim—right through my trousers . . . *(They grin)* A proper— bollock-splitter . . . *(He goes on, with effort)* A fart—to—rot my pants— and—blow—the worms across—the shithouse—wall . . . *(Pause)*

DITCH *(cupping a hand to his ear).* Can't 'ear nothing. *(Pause. MUSIC comes up to PAIN, stands behind him)*

PAIN. Oh, God, this is an awful place, and in their bronzed and burning beauty all my sin laps me with tongues of shame . . .

ISTED. Come again.

DITCH. Didn't know you spoke Chinese.

MUSIC. *(turning on them).* Fuck off.

ISTED. Oh, dear.

MUSIC. Fuck off.

DITCH. Look, can we just—

MUSIC. Just get off! *(They look to PAIN, who does not respond to them. Sheepishly, they depart, watched by MUSIC)* If the desert opened up and swallowed 'em, their mothers would not weep a sparrow's wee-wee . . .

PAIN. No.

MUSIC. Look at 'em, hovering like a pack of dewdrops in search of an old man's nose. How the khaki dignifies. In a dancehall you could bump their prissy elbows and they would apologize . . .

PAIN. I have never been in a dancehall.

MUSIC. Well, you don't eat skirt, do you?

PAIN. No.

MUSIC. We are a mincing little race. The trilling and the traipsing to some ninny's trumpet just to get your finger up some sad bint's slit.

PAIN. You have to drink. If you have a thirst, you have to drink, for all you lucidity.

MUSIC. I 'ave demolished bars and barmen in my flashes. I 'ave sent mirrors and little men with combs to shattery, bumped and fucked my life away under the Locarno's glitter. And look at you. Wise. Little. Perfect. Still. I 'ave such an arse-aching envy of a bloke like you. I could crack your brainbox.

PAIN. Yes. I know. *(Pause)*

MUSIC. All right. Tell me about the bastard Caesar.

ERICA *comes in, followed by* PORCELAIN *pushing an* OLD MAN *in a wheelchair. The* SOLDIERS *stand.*

ERICA. He wants to see the sea.

MUSIC. The sea is very good today, sir! *(He takes a kneeling position beside the chair, points out to sea)* High and thrusting. Like 'er breasts.

TALLBOY. What did he say?

MUSIC. Rolling and plunging. Like 'er arse.

TALLBOY. What?

ERICA. Would anyone like the binoculars?

PAIN. 'ear the suck of it! Like 'er lips on your pleaser.

TALLBOY.   What is he saying?

ERICA.   Not a bit like Cornwall, he says. (*She turns to* PAIN) This is Mr Porcelain. Mr Porcelain has come from London. He is with the Water Board.

PORCELAIN.   I believe we've met.

ERICA.   You are to render Mr Porcelain every conceivable assistance. He is writing a report.

PORCELAIN.   On water.

PAIN.   There is no water here.

PORCELAIN.   So Miss Tallboy tells me.

ERICA.   That should not deter him from writing a report.

PAIN.   It comes by pipe. The army guards the pipe. The pipe waters the army.

PORCELAIN.   Yes.

PAIN.   Without the pipe you couldn't have the army. Without the army you couldn't have the pipe.

PORCELAIN.   Quite.

PAIN.   The symmetry of Empire.

ERICA.   Mr Porcelain has never been abroad before.

MUSIC.   This is not abroad. I would not dignify this by the name abroad. Abroad is cold beer and wops with trays. We are completely wopless 'ere. As for trays, 'ave you ever seen one? The beer is 'ot and you carry it yourself. They tried to show a film 'ere once, but it melted in the gate.

ERICA.   I am taking dad to the water. He wants to dip his feet. (*She looks at* MUSIC) Perhaps you'd push?

MUSIC *pushes the wheelchair off.* PORCELAIN *watches them go. Pause.*

PORCELAIN.   Not really water.

PAIN.   What?

PORCELAIN.   Me.

PAIN.   Not water?

PORCELAIN.   No. (*Pause.* PAIN *looks at him*)

PAIN.   Ah. What, then?

PORCELAIN.   Can't tell you.

PAIN.   Oh, go on.

PORCELAIN.   No. Better not.

PAIN.   Well, please yourself. *(He turns to go away)*

PORCELAIN.   Confidential Evaluation of the Governor.

PAIN   *(stopping).* I see.

PORCELAIN.   Forget I told you.

PAIN.   Yes, all right.

PORCELAIN.   Have you?

PAIN.   Nearly. *(He passes his hand across his eyes)* Gone.

PORCELAIN.   Good. I so hate lies. And I don't know anything about water.

PAIN.   Difficult assignment.

PORCELAIN.   Yes. What's more. I miss my mother.

PAIN.   Do you? So do I.

PORCELAIN. You do?

PAIN. Desperately.

PORCELAIN. You must love her very much.

PAIN. She conceived me in an alleyway in Aberdeen, up against a lamp-post. A difficult position, she informed me, but greatly appreciated by my father. He had a mansion with three hundred bedrooms and had grown very contemptuous of the horizontal. My mother was a parlour maid, bred for taking upright between the kitchen and the bath. They had eight children. I am a genius, the rest are simple. Probably she conceived them on her back.

PORCELAIN. I don't suppose, if you happen to have an evening, you'd care to sit and talk about our mums?

PAIN. You know, I've never done that.

PORCELAIN. Nor have I, what do you think?

PAIN *(after a moment's thought)*. No. It would be like girls discussing lovers. We'd only want to hear about our own. (PAIN *turns to go*)

PORCELAIN. The thing is . . . (PAIN *stops*) I'm never going to see her again.

PAIN. Oh?

PORCELAIN. One of us is dying.

PAIN. Which?

PORCELAIN. I don't know yet. (*Pause.* PAIN *looks at him*) I can't bring myself to unpack my bag. Because she packed it. She has a way of packing bags. I have been wearing the same clothes for a week.

PAIN. I'll lend you a pair of socks.

PORCELAIN. Thank you. *(Pause)*

PAIN. Don't be afraid of dying.

PORCELAIN. I am.

PAIN. When you have seen a lot of dying, it forfeits all its mystery. It is not like killing, which is fine and proper done in ecstasy. Dying is dull, a fitting ending to a thing itself dull. Try to be killed. I do.

He walks away as MUSIC *reappears pushing the wheelchair at a run. The old man is roaring.*

MUSIC. Oh, Sir 'arry! Sir 'arry Tallboy! What 'ave they done to 'im?

ERICA *(hurrying after)*. You nearly drowned him!

MUSIC *(pretending to fuss)*. The naughty wave! The wave would up and after 'im! The wave would not lie down, would it? I said this is a man who 'olds 'is title from a king, down wave, get down you yobby wave, you, but no, it comes and slops 'im round the chops!

ERICA. Get away from him.

MUSIC. Shall I press 'is rib cage? RESPIRATION 'ere!

ERICA. YOU ARE SUFFOCATING HIM!

MUSIC *(moving away)*. Waves. Punishment of. Ten rounds rapid. Fire!

TALLBOY. Oh, what have they done to me?

MUSIC *(saluting)*. Waves accounted for, sir!

ERICA *(To* MUSIC*)*. Listen. You grab too much. For what you give. You grab too much. *(He stares at her)* Mr Porcelain, don't stand there, please!

PORCELAIN *(hurrying over).*   What shall I—
ERICA.   Remove his trousers! Dry his feet!
TALLBOY.   I never want to see the sea again . . .
ERICA.   Oh, don't say that.
TALLBOY.   It tried to murder me . . .
MUSIC *(to* PORCELAIN).   When we first came 'ere, I could point to England, worked it out with compass and a map. *(He points off)* Two thousand miles from the tip of my finger to the door 'andles of the Elephant, two thousand from this clinker to the baking pavement of the Old Kent Road, desert to desert, drought to drought. Then rumour started that it wasn't there, that they 'ad sold or shifted it. Why else would they not give us leave? True, during the war we were considered unreliable, running from gunfire and passing round leaflets scattered by the enemy. But the war is over, and still we 'ave no leave. Rumour goes on to say England's so sad they are afraid to let us look at it . . .
ERICA *(leaving* TALLBOY).   You are arrested.
MUSIC.   Again? And charged with what?
ERICA.   Bringing the person of the Governor into danger.
MUSIC.   Two days' loss of privilege.
ERICA.   Failure to protect the King's representative.
MUSIC.   Two more.
ERICA.   Acting in a manner likely to harm the safety of the Colony.
MUSIC.   And two makes six. Now kiss my arse to make the sentence stick.
ERICA.   Go to the camp and place yourself under arrest.
MUSIC *(making towards her).*   All right, I will kiss yours.
ERICA.   Do not touch me. Or I will have you shot. *(Pause)*
MUSIC.   You think you are so special.
ERICA.   Yes.
MUSIC.   You even 'ave the brass to think you're beautiful.
ERICA.   Yes. You have muttered it to me often enough.
MUSIC.   You are like the pre-war Guinness that was washed up on the beach last week. The buggers 'ad not seen one for so many years they squabbled even though the stuff was stinking stale. In times of scarcity even a mouthwash passes for champagne . . .
TALLBOY.   Erica!
ERICA.   Yes.
TALLBOY.   Home! Home!
MUSIC.   I should not 'ave said that.
ERICA.   No. You shouldn't have.
MUSIC.   All right, I—
ERICA *(going away from him).*   Mr Porcelain, come on!
PORCELAIN *(struggling with the chair).*   I'm sorry, it—
ERICA.   You will never grow to be strong!

She joins him, they push the wheelchair away, watched ruefully by MUSIC. TOPLIS *appears, with juggling balls. Pause.*

TOPLIS. Who is she?

MUSIC *(turning, slowly)*. Who are you?

TOPLIS *(throwing up the balls)*. A tickler of the imagination, Eddie Music.

MUSIC. Are you? Well, tickle mine. 'ow do you know my name?

TOPLIS. Is your name so very private, private?

MUSIC. I care who uses it.

TOPLIS *(catching the balls, putting them away, and looking at* MUSIC*)*. What became of your sergeant's stripes?

MUSIC. They dropped off in a battle, and I never picked 'em up again.

TOPLIS. Like that, was it? *(He walks a little way, hands in pockets)* This is a flinty place, Eddie. No moisture. And a sun to dry the juice out of the randiest slit. Shoving in a bag of crisps would yield more pleasure. Who did you say she was?

MUSIC. I didn't. And lay off the Eddie. I am not Eddie to a monkey in a yellow suit.

TOPLIS *(unperturbed, gazing about him)*. To think so many fluttering scraps of English youth squealed and twitched to get this place. So much blood, bursting out of darkness through shot veins. Blood used to alleys and saloon bars, to shaving cuts at most . . .

MUSIC. It's strategic.

TOPLIS. Strategic, is it?

Pause. TOPLIS *turns to face* MUSIC.

TOPLIS. I have spent three years in French hotels. Hotels where they have plates to take the plate your plate goes on, and napkins made to crack like pistols in the dining room. Hotels where the air is thick as carpet and the carpet drowns your feet. Where the stillness is like the stillness of a bottled embryo, such stillness you can hear the rasping of a waiter's fingers at his balls. Where the hiss of silk on silk, of knicker sliding under slip, and slip sliding over stocking, is the very roar of life. Where passion is a corridor of spunk-stained linen. *(Pause)* Of course a man plumps up a bit. So many croissants! Croissant and a fuck. Fuck and a croissant. A man can't help but put on flesh. Especially a dead one. *(Pause)* What is it? The sun? (MUSIC *is shuddering. His hands go to his face. He sobs)* Oh, there, there . . . there, there . . . *(He goes to touch him.* MUSIC *pulls away)*

MUSIC. Fuck you . . .

TOPLIS. Yes . . .

MUSIC. Fuck you!

TOPLIS. Quite.

MUSIC. Oh, fuck you . . .

TOPLIS. Well, this is a welcome.

MUSIC. I wept for you.

TOPLIS. Yes.

MUSIC. Beat my 'ead against the wall for you!

TOPLIS. That was more than kind, Eddie.

MUSIC. Oh, shuddup!

TOPLIS. Well, what am I supposed to—

MUSIC. Shuddup. (*Pause. Eventually* MUSIC *looks up*) You look a spunk bag in that suit.

TOPLIS. Tight on the arms . . . (*Pause.* MUSIC *is groping for comprehension*)

MUSIC. Three years in where?

TOPLIS. Deauville.

MUSIC. Never 'eard of it.

TOPLIS. It's a place rich women go to smother their misery. (MUSIC *looks at him, coldly*) I wanted to live, Eddie. To eat, and drink, and lie in starched sheets with clean, thin women. I wanted to wear bright shirts and patent shoes, and nurse my lovely body, free of dirt and yelling, drape it on a balcony, the smartest balcony my wits could buy . . . (*Pause*)

MUSIC. And me?

TOPLIS. I did not give one thought to you.

MUSIC. No.

TOPLIS: Not one. (*Pause*) I was twelve hours in the guardroom. With two sergeants. In cold like death. And from the bottom of myself, up from the sump of all my life, through shit and through despair, I drew up words, I sucked up sentences so pure and so magic they pulled their balaclavas off their ears. Out of the little piss-puddle that I was, I moved their pity, word after beaten, bleeding word. HAVE YOU EVER SPOKEN FOR TWELVE HOURS!

MUSIC. No. (*Pause*)

TOPLIS. It comes to me in dreams. No barrage we were under makes me shrink like all those words. (*Pause*) I lived, you see. I lived. When they came to tie me to the post, while the squad were stamping in the snow, I was not there. Nor my sergeants neither. My sergeants who had blood on their greatcoats from the murder of deserters . . . (*Pause*)

MUSIC. Toplis is lying in an unmarked grave, they said.

TOPLIS. A good lie's near enough the truth. I was in no-man's land, with krauts and jocks, greybeards who sprächt half Glasgow, hälfte Dusseldorf. We advanced with the Great Advance and retreated with the Great Retreat. Or vice versa. Anyway, we lived. I was lying in a Countess when they blew the armistice. (*Pause. They look at one another*)

MUSIC. I don't get what—

TOPLIS. Ask me to dance for you.

MUSIC. Why you—

TOPLIS. Ask me. I love the tap.

MUSIC. Listen!

TOPLIS. Since you press me—(*He begins to perform a tap routine*) I did this on the Riviera.

MUSIC. Look, don't be a cunt!

TOPLIS. Eddie, this is for you!

MUSIC. DON'T DANCE! I 'ATE DANCING!

TOPLIS. Hate dancing? How can anyone hate dancing?

MUSIC. I'M 'APPY 'ERE! WHY DO YOU 'AVE TO SPOIL IT WHEN I'M 'APPY 'ERE?

TOPLIS.   No, no. *(He stops, in a tap posture)* Not happy here. *(Pause)* Not happy because you are not free.

MUSIC.   Go away. Please, Michael. Go away.

Pause, then black.

Scene Three

The Governor's House. A table and chairs. DITCH *stands stiffly in a waiter's jacket.*

DITCH.   Why is it when we think of 'er, we think of blood? Think bayonets between 'er tits and rifle barrels in 'er cunt? Think murder of a sort? Stan says 'e's looked at 'er when carving and shook with wanting to slit 'er from tit to rump . . . *(Pause)* Oh, I 'ope she does not ask me can I do 'er 'ook and eye. Stan says she arches when 'e docs 'er 'ook and eye so 'is gaze travels down the valley of 'er spine to where the arse rises. I 'ope she does not ask me do 'er 'ook and eye!

ERICA *enters, looks at him.*

ERICA.   Thinking bloody thoughts again?

DITCH.   No, Miss.

ERICA.   Don't want to stick the carving fork up my vagina?

DITCH.   No, Miss, thank you very much.

ERICA.   Good. *(She goes to the table, begins, moving chairs)*

DITCH.   Oh, Miss . . .

ERICA.   Yes?

DITCH.   Er.

ERICA.   What?

DITCH.   The 'ook and eye.

ERICA.   What about it?

DITCH.   Do it, shall I?

ERICA.   Thank you. It's already done.

DITCH.   Undo it, then. *(Pause. She looks at him)*

ERICA.   No. *(He looks hurt)*

DITCH.   I WON ELEVEN GAMES OF PONTOON TO BE 'ERE TONIGHT! *(Pause)*

HACKER *comes in, groomed.*

HACKER.   Miss Tallboy, this is an honour!

ERICA   *(taking his hand).* Mr Hacker.

HACKER.   I should 'ave brought some flowers but there are no flowers to be 'ad, so I looked for chocolates, but failed to make myself understood. Black Magic is something to do with toads and sheep's eyes, apparently. I give you instead, in all humility, a chit, redeemable at my own store. *(He gives her an envelope)*

ERICA.   Oh, what a beautiful chit! Should it be put in water, do you think?

HACKER.   By all means, though the ink might run . . .

ERICA (*handing it to* ISTED). You do it. (*She pours* HACKER *a drink*) How are you enjoying the country, Mr Hacker?

HACKER. I thought it beautiful the moment the coast hove into view. Beautiful with opportunity. Beautiful with nothingness waiting for somethingness to 'appen. (*He takes the glass*) Thank you. (*He sips*) This is sheer delight. 'o is supplying you? (*He lifts the bottle out of the ice bucket*)

DITCH (*coming to attention*). The Governor! (TALLBOY *enters, pushed by* PORCELAIN)

TALLBOY. Where's the magician?

ERICA. Not here yet.

TALLBOY. I want the magician!

ERICA. You will have to be patient.

TALLBOY. I want a trick! I want a trick!

ERICA. You will see plenty of tricks, I promise you.

PORCELAIN. Mrs Struggle not here yet?

HACKER. Mrs Struggle 'as set 'er face against the services I offer. She'd walk the 'eels off 'er shoes before she'd travel in my taxi. Unfortunately for Mrs Struggle, I am now the sole importer of ladies' shoes. Eventually I will be the only source of 'aberdashery. No woman will walk without my label in 'er drawers.

ERICA. You have such lofty aspirations, Mr Hacker.

HACKER. No, but I will 'ave my triumph. Every man must 'ave 'is triumph. Is it my fault I'm not a poet sitting caressing 'is ankles? No, it's not. I 'ave no gifts, but I am not afraid of effort. There is not enough appreciation of effort in this world. Ain't that so, Mr Porcelain?

PORCELAIN. I like poetry myself.

HACKER. Like it by all means. Rub it in yer rheumatism. All I say is, there's no more credit due to poetry than effort. Christ, man, you are effort as ever was, you poor bloody struggler.

PORCELAIN. I do my best.

HACKER. Not everything is done with ease and grace, is it, Sir Harry? I shit with effort, not with grace. 'ow do you shit, Mr Porcelain?

PORCELAIN. I—

ERICA. How did we get on to this?

HACKER. I dunno. Somebody mocked me. (*He sits down, undoes his tie*) Christ, it's 'ot . . . (ISTED *ushers in* THREE WOMEN)

ISTED. Mrs Struggle and 'er party, sir!

STRUGGLE (*surging forward*). Miss Tallboy, I presume?

ERICA. Good evening.

STRUGGLE. May I introduce Miss Trellis? And Miss Knotting?

TALLBOY. Which is the magician?

ERICA. No, daddy, these ladies are prostitutes.

STRUGGLE. PROSTITUTES.

ERICA. Oh, aren't you—

STRUGGLE. PROSTITUTES.

ERICA. I beg your pardon. These ladies are not prostitutes.

STRUGGLE. Not PROSTITUTES.

ERICA (*to* ISTED). Give the not prostitutes a drink, will you? (*To the* WOMEN) do take a seat. What a beautiful dress!

STRUGGLE. The word, Miss Tallboy.

ERICA. The word?

STRUGGLE. We are in the hands of words.

ERICA. Yes.

STRUGGLE. Woman is a word. Are you not a woman?

ERICA. I have been led to think so.

STRUGGLE. Yet I have heard men utter it with such an effluence of saliva and snittering teeth you would have thought wasps were clinging to the inside of their mouths.

ERICA (*turning away*). Where is this man?

TALLBOY. Will he cut a tart in half?

ERICA (*to* ISTED). Look for him, will you?

TALLBOY. HE'S GOT TO CUT A TART IN HALF!

ERICA. I'm sure he will.

PORCELAIN. I don't really see the skill in that . . .

HACKER. 'e means a woman, stupid.

KNOTTING. Miss Tallboy, can I ask you something?

STRUGGLE. Oh, dear. Jane has this notion. She is prey to notions, aren't you, Jane?

KNOTTING. This ain't a notion.

STRUGGLE. It is a notion, silly. You were in the grip of it when I discovered you at Aldershot.

KNOTTING. I was wrong, then.

STRUGGLE. And you are wrong now.

ERICA. I'm sure we're all agog to know what Miss Knotting's notion is. (*Pause*)

KNOTTING. Miss Tallboy, have I seen Lawrence of Arabia? (*Pause*)

ERICA. I find that rather hard to answer. What do people who have seen him look like?

KNOTTING. Well, I 'ave.

ERICA. You have?

KNOTTING. Definitely. Yes, I 'ave.

ERICA. So why are you asking me? (*Pause*)

KNOTTING. Sorry. Start again. I 'ave seen Lawrence of Arabia, 'aven't I? (*Pause*) I saw 'im on the beach the morning we arrived, but never said nothing. And then I saw 'im later, walking up and down outside our tent, doing the shall–I–shan't–I shuffle, looking at the boys come in, and I said Lawrence of Arabia!

STRUGGLE. Not for the first time.

KNOTTING. Maybe not.

STRUGGLE. She has identified him in a dozen army camps.

KNITTING. So what?

STRUGGLE. Pirbright. Shorncliffe. Catterick.

KNOTTING. All right!

STRUGGLE. Bought her a drink, she says.

KNOTTING.   Well, yes 'e did! A cherry brandy!
STRUGGLE.   A corporal in the tanks, this is.
KNOTTING.   That's right, so what?
STRUGGLE.   LAWRENCE OF ARABIA?
KNOTTING.   It was!
STRUGGLE.   And then he said—
KNOTTING.   Shuddup, Struggle.
STRUGGLE.   He said—
KNOTTING.   NEVER TELL YOU ANYTHING AGAIN.
STRUGGLE.   Buy her knickers for a quid. *(Pause)*
ERICA.   And did you sell them?
KNOTTING.   No. *(Pause)* I gave 'em to 'im. It was Lawrence of Arabia, wasn't it?
ISTED *(entering)*.   Mr Toplis, conjuror!
TOPLIS *(entering in a black cloak, clasping a small bag)*.   Greetings from the pool of darkness! My humble credentials as ambassador of the arcane I lay before you! *(He bows)*
ERICA.   You're late.
TOPLIS.   I was in consultation with the powers of the night.
ERICA.   This is Government House. No one is allowed to be late. You would not be late for the king. This is the king.
TALLBOY.   GOT TO CUT A TART IN HALF!
ERICA.   Do you require the lights switched off?
HACKER.   Love yer outfit, Toplis. Where d'yer scrounge clobber like that?
TOPLIS *(placing his bag on the table)*.   Kindly do not distract the magician.
HACKER.   Must 'ave nicked it. 'is bag was no bigger than a Scotch wallet.
TOPLIS.   I drew unto myself the energy of Dis, and lo, he delivered me that which I needed for my purpose.
HACKER.   Luvvly. Give 'im a drink.
TALLBOY.   BE QUIET!
HACKER.   Sorry.
TOPLIS.   I must ask for your complete attention, please. Lower the lights.
TALLBOY *(as ISTED switches off most of the lights)*.   Got to saw the tart in half. . .
ERICA.   My father wants to see a woman sawn into two.
TOPLIS.   It is my intention to divide a woman here tonight.
ERICA.   Good.
TOPLIS.   Gather round the table, please. Not too close, and not too distant, sufficient for the discharge of emotion and the flow of pure thought—*(They form a semi-circle of chairs in front of TOPLIS' table)* Thought unencumbered, thought so simple, so spontaneous and childlike it will charm the air—put your cigar out, please—*(HACKER stubs out his cigar)* and watch my eyes—watch them—do I not have the eyes of one who has seen to the very soul of things?
TALLBOY.   Yes!
TOPLIS.   Who has been granted one glance at the Absolute and been so blasted that it scorched the tunnels of his eyes?
TALLBOY.   Yes!

TOPLIS.   Listen, then. Magic is Truth, and Truth is Magic. Once I walked in the darkness, crashing like a stranger in a darkened room, bruised by this and grazed by that, my fingertips insensitive from handling common things, blind with looking, sick with touching loveless flesh, my mouth stale with the shared opinion—*(Pause)* Do not move your chair, please. I require complete attention—*(Pause)* Your eyes on mine. Thank you *(Pause)* The led me up to Death, showed Death to me to make me tremble, but Death pitied me, saying him I will not take, though he wears no shoulder badges nor crowns upon his sleeve, him will I share my magic with because he has a back to bear the truth, which is a mighty burden and cuts the bearer off from love of men, though not of women—*(Pause)* Someone coughed—

TALLBOY.   Don't cough!

TOPLIS.   My magic will spill continents, set pavements shaking and splash blood in the flower beds, but I will save you, spare you from the pain of painlessness, the half-fuck and the semi-anger, the endless rattle of your questions which are not questions, I will uncover you and you will say I never knew I was so beautiful, I will separate your clothes and set the tired flesh free, I show you magic, I show you magic—(ERICA, *as if in a trance, rises to her feet, and unbuttoning her dress, tears it from her shoulders, exposing her breasts)* I show you—I show you—*(He reaches swiftly into his open bag and takes out a revolver. He fires a blank into the ceiling.* ERICA *starts)* Thank you! Thank you! *(She runs out of the room)* Thank you!

HACKER.   What in Christ's name—

TOPLIS *(putting the revolver away)*.   Thank you—

STRUGGLE.   Was she—

HACKER.   Come on, Toplis—

TALLBOY.   DO IT AGAIN! I WAS ASLEEP!

KNOTTING.   Don't see the trick.

TALLBOY.   DO IT AGAIN!

KNOTTING.   That's not a trick.

TOPLIS.   Who said anything about tricks? I don't deal in tricks. I deal in magic.

HACKER.   Magic's tricks!

TOPLIS.   On the contrary, magic is truth, and like truth, only penetrates where it knows it will be welcome.

HACKER.   Balls. *(He looks to* TALLBOY*)* Beg pardon. *(To Ditch)* come on, son, watch the glasses!

STRUGGLE.   Did you feel—what she—

KNOTTING.   No.

HACKER.   Come on, Toplis, we want a rabbit and an 'at.

TALLBOY.   DO IT AGAIN. (ERICA *comes in, properly clothed*)

ERICA.   Thank you. We shall not be requiring any more.

TOPLIS *(bowing)*.   As you wish.

TALLBOY.   DO IT AGAIN!

ERICA.   Mr Toplis is leaving.

TALLBOY.   No!

ERICA.   Good night.

TOPLIS *(taking his bag).* Miss Tallboy has spared me the embarrassment of confessing I have no further variations on my act.

HACKER. Say that again!

TALLBOY. Come again! Do come again! (TOPLIS *bows again, withdraws*)

ERICA *(to* TALLBOY). Come on, time for bed.

TALLBOY. No!

ERICA *(nodding to* PORCELAIN *and* ISTED). I will come up and read you a story. (*They wheel the* OLD MAN *out.* ERICA *looks at* TRELLIS) I wonder, when the others go, if you would care to stay behind?

TRELLIS. Me?

ERICA. Yes. Please. *(She turns to them)* Thank you for coming. My father loves a little company. *(She calls)* Coats, Ditch!

HACKER *(draining his glass, leaping to his feet).* Your father obviously tires easily. I 'ope we 'ave not kept 'im up.

ERICA. Government is a debilitating business. (DITCH *hands* HACKER *his straw hat. He takes* ERICA'S *hand*) Good night.

The TWO WOMEN *curtsy. They all leave, but for* TRELLIS, *standing nervously.* ERICA *drapes herself over a chair, looks at her. Pause.*

ERICA. I must say when you arrived I was very angry. I was livid. Look how young you are! I was the object of all their frantic gloats and secret rubbing. My underwear, my knickers in particular, were stolen from the line. I was obliged to go knickerless, they had my knickers on under their khaki shorts, and if they could steal them from the basket, fresh from my crutch, all the better! They were auctioned, passed down, my stain pressed against a whole battaillion's lips! *(pause)* Since you arrived I find I have all the pairs I want. I must say that took some getting over. *(Pause. She leaps up)* Come on, let's have a drink! Let's have a piss-up, shall we? *(She fills two glasses, hands one to* TRELLIS) What's he like? The magician? Have you had him? Does he look ashamed or murderous? I prefer the look of murder, I do want to be murdered, do you? Not in the morning. That's different. In the morning I hate to be touched. What did you say?

TRELLIS. Me?

ERICA. Yes.

TRELLIS. No—

ERICA. In the morning I just wash and wash. Have you noticed their cocks in the morning? Slack, uncurling, rolling to a little bit of dirty dream. Fill up your glass. Go on. *(She goes reluctantly to the ice-bucket)* I have ambiguous feelings towards circumcision. Do you like them circumcised? Oh, come on, you are so pretty, what do you say?

TRELLIS. I—

ERICA. Cocks, come on!

TRELLIS. I—

ERICA. Yes? *(Pause)* Look, if you are going to be my best friend I do think we will have to talk. What's the point in having a best friend if she doesn't say anything! *(She gets up, fills her glass, clumsily)* What do you do with soft ones? Do you stuff them in? Like shoving pate in a chicken's arse?

TRELLIS. I never seen one. (*Pause.* ERICA *looks at her*)
ERICA. Never—
TRELLIS.No. *(Pause)*
ERICA. But—
TRELLIS. I shut my eyes.
ERICA. You shut your eyes. Is that working-class? To shut your eyes? (TRELLIS *starts to go*) Don't go! *(She stops)* You are my best friend. Please don't go! *(Pause)* You are so pretty, but I don't envy you, honestly I don't. I am raddled and forty and you are lovely and twenty, but I don't envy you. That's good, isn't it? *(Pause. She wanders nervously around)* I have to tell you when he started all that gibberish I thought I am going to show my tits. I did. I was not taken in one little bit. But it seemed the perfect opportunity to show him my tits. Did you want to show him yours?
TRELLIS. Nope.
ERICA. No? I really did. I have seen him naked, you see, and I wanted him to see me, too. *(She turns)* Where, did you say? On the beach. I forced him naked. And I must say I could have licked him all over. Have you had him?
TRELLIS. I think I better—
ERICA. Suppose I hadn't done it? What would he have done? Nothing, I suppose . . . *(She puts her glass down)* Thank you for talking to me. I would love to coax you, but I haven't time. Life's so short, isn't it? Especially at forty. You are still my best friend, obviously. I have no others.

She drapes the coat over her shoulders. TRELLIS *leaves.* ERICA *drops into the chair. A man appears behind her.*

PAIN. I let myself in. Am I keeping you up?
ERICA. No. I am so tense I could box with a gorilla.
PAIN. I'll box with you.
ERICA. I feel as though there is no substance in me, only tension. No flesh, just energy. I float. I shudder.
PAIN. Where are the boxing gloves?
ERICA *(jumping out of her chair).* Thank God you came. Or I should have dragged the little civil servant out of bed and beaten him. *(She pulls boxing-gloves out of a drawer, tosses a pair to him)* No rules!
PAIN. No rules.
ERICA. I hate rules! Murder the rules!
PAIN. The essence of government is the establishment of rules which the governor himself has no intention of keeping. Universal approbation of principles like justice, law, democracy—
ERICA *(swiping at him).* DING!
PAIN *(ducking).* suffuse the mass consciousness, enabling the governors to practise duplicity to their heart's content—
ERICA. YOU ARE NOT ALLOWED TO RUN AWAY!
PAIN. That is a rule!
ERICA *(pursuing him).* I WANT TO HIT YOU!
PAIN. Ah, yes.
ERICA. LET ME HIT YOU!
PAIN *(trapped).* DING!

ERICA.   That wasn't three minutes!

PAIN.   No rules!

ERICA *(hitting him in the jaw)*.   DING! Left hook!

PAIN.   I fall . . .

ERICA.   Followed by—upper cut . . .

PAIN *(collapsing)*.   I bleed . . .

ERICA.   I go on hitting you!

PAIN.   I moan . . .

ERICA.   I love it!

PAIN.   I plead . . .

ERICA *(sitting astride him)*.   I still don't stop!

PAIN.   I DIE.

ERICA.   Oh, no!

PAIN *(head to one side)*.   A fleck of foam hangs on my lips . . .

ERICA *(no longer hitting him)*.   Bore.

PAIN.   A sepulchral whiteness glimmers through his sunburned skin . . . white as a girl's where collar kept it from the sun . . . but girl-free . . . girl-innocent . . .

ERICA.   Why do you always have to die?

PAIN.   Rots . . . rots . . . rots . . .

ERICA.   Seriously, why do you always have to die? Very few boxers actually die. In the ring. It's very rare. *(She gets up, tosses off her gloves)* I'm fed up with you dying. *(She slumps in a chair)* It's very late. Why are you here?

PAIN.   Do you enjoy a paradox?

ERICA.   I don't know. What is a paradox?

PAIN.   Here's one. A conjuror who drops the playing-cards. A juggler who cannot keep three balls aloft. A hypnotist who cannot stare.

ERICA.   I know the one.

PAIN.   So bad an entertainer, yet so entertaining. Such a tawdry talent, yet has the loutish English soldiers stand on chairs. He could not produce a single rabbit, but they did not even touch their beer . . . *(Pause)* What is his charm?

ERICA *(disingenuously)*.   I can't think.

PAIN.   I will tell you. He has Moscow magic. Learned at the Diabolical Academy of Dr Marx.

ERICA.   Who?

PAIN.   Marx, a pedant.

ERICA.   Never heard of him.

PAIN.   Dr Marx has given soldiers a philosophical authority for doing what they only had an instinct for. Shooting their officers. I want you to arrest him.

ERICA.   On what grounds? Insufficient rabbits?

PAIN.   Deport him and they will meet him at the docks. *(Pause. She gets up, walks a little way, stops)*

ERICA.   Well, thank you. Now I think I'll go to bed.

PAIN.   Don't you want to ring the police?

ERICA.   The police?

PAIN.   Yes.
ERICA.   Now?
PAIN.   Why not? *(Pause)*
ERICA.   It's awfully late. *(Pause. He stares at her)* Well, isn't it? *(He stares)* Will you not look at me like that? *(He stares)* I have to discuss it with the Governor! *(Pause, then he gets up, prepares to leave)*
PAIN.   One night like this, a full moon like—how would a modern poet put it—like spittle on a financier's astrakhan—I walked into a gully, full of flowers and the dead. The Arabs had stripped them naked, and their skin glowed, glistening with dew. I smoothed their limbs, and drew their eyelids closed. And then, finding I had come erect, stripped off my robe and lay among them, breathing like a star and stiff with cold . . . *(Pause)* You and I, we are so weak for flesh . . .

He smiles, goes out. Blackout.

Scene Four

HACKER *is pushing a handcart with three empty coffins on it. He is watched by* STRUGGLE, TRELLIS *and* KNOTTING.

HACKER.   Shall I reserve one for you, ladies? The civilian casket is of similar construction but the handles are of brass. You would lie beautifully in one of these, they are generous in proportion, wide where the common casket's narrow. They have to be, of course. The swelling is monstrous in this heat.
STRUGGLE.   I would not put it past you to have brought typhus to this place.
HACKER.   Alas, bacteriology is not among my skills.
STRUGGLE.   Peculiar, on the outbreak, Hacker has access to wood. Where wood cannot be found. Where the army drops 'em down in blankets, Hacker can lay hands on timber.
HACKER.   I could say lucky, but I won't. I do not believe in luck, I believe in preparation. *(He picks up the handles of the cart)* I must get on, or my three faces will be too fat for the box. Faces you 'ave fondled, ladies. I 'ope I do not see you grinning dead. Are you sure you won't place a reservation?
STRUGGLE.   I would be stinking jelly before I went into one of your crates.
HACKER.   What a thing pride is! Scraped off your bed with shovels. And you so very strong on dignity! Is your will written? I am the sole importer of testaments.

TOPLIS *appears with* THREE SOLDIERS.
TOPLIS.   Death rate satisfactory, Mr Hacker?
HACKER.   Well, I could wish the epidemic had a bit more grip. *(He screws his face into a sneer)* You are a sniveller, Toplis. It's a good thing I am 'ere. The government 'as no facilities. *(He turns to go)*
TOPLIS.   Don't go! I have three likely customers!

HACKER. These caskets is booked.

TOPLIS. We'll pay over them. They're in no condition to bid.

HACKER. Let a geezer do 'is job.

TOPLIS *(blocking his way)*. Anybody want to try one?

HACKER. Come on, lads, your captain turned to water in this 'eat . . .

ISTED *(fingering a coffin)*. A very thin material . . .

TOPLIS. To let the wearer breathe, no doubt.

DITCH. I'll try one on. Measure my inside leg.

HACKER. Oh, blimey. I 'ave fallen among the wits. (*The* SOLDIERS *begin unloading a coffin*) YOU'RE 'OLDING UP SOMEBODY'S FUNERAL! *(He turns to the women)* Ladies, 'ow about employing your good offices? I've 'eard the female touch can soften yobbery. DON'T SNAP THE LIDS!

KNOTTING. I wanna stand in a coffin!

DITCH *(grabbing her round the waist)*. Kiss me, mother!

ISTED *(pulling another off the cart)*. Tim–ber!

HACKER. I WILL 'AVE YOU LOT!

TOPLIS. Miss Trellis, have you made love in a coffin?

STRUGGLE. Don't go with him. He hasn't twopence to close his eyelids with.

TOPLIS. Coffins should be baptized with a little pleasure. They have such a long time in the dark, and the occupant's knees come up so slowly . . .

KNOTTING *(lying in a coffin)*. Peace . . . perfect peace . . . (DITCH *climbs on top of her*) Who's this?

DITCH. The Angel Gabriel.

KNOTTING. The Angel Gabriel?

HACKER. What are your numbers? Give me your numbers!

KNOTTING. The Angel Gabriel's got his hands up me!

HACKER (*to* ISTED). I know you! You was the waiter at the 'ouse.

TOPLIS. Will no one kiss me?

ISTED. I will kiss you.

TOPLIS (*to* STRUGGLE). You see, I have made friends . . .

HACKER. I stand amazed. I am struck as if by lightning. What is the British army coming to? I 'ave been ambushed and my goods waylaid. You cannot rule the lesser breeds without superiority. WHERE IS YOUR FUCKING SUPERIORITY?

TOPLIS. Where are the lesser breeds?

HACKER. I begin to wonder. YOU 'AVE BUSTED THAT!

DITCH. We are the lesser breeds, ain't we?

HACKER. Many a true word—

ISTED. WE ARE VERY LESSER! VERY LESSER WE ARE!

HACKER. You 'ave your boots on somebody's plate . . .

DITCH. The spittle of a rich man's threat, we are. *(Pause)*

HACKER. Toplis 'as been on at you.

ISTED. We won't see England again. And good riddance to it.

HACKER. My feelings exactly. The last thing I left in England was my spit. Gobbed it from the boat deck, saw it glisten on the quay. My florin of contempt.

DITCH. We make it here.

HACKER. Make what?

TOPLIS. England. In our fashion.

ISTED. No fields for hunting through. No churches for apologizing in. No filth. No judges. No wit. *(Pause)*

HACKER. What is this?

TOPLIS. Hurry up. Your officers will have burst and flung their tatters down the beach . . .

HACKER. WHAT'S 'E SAYING? *(Pause, then the* SOLDIERS *start flinging the coffins back on the cart)*

DITCH. Get up!

ISTED. Gee up, you mare!

TOPLIS. You abject undertaker. RUN!

HACKER *(struck by the flat of* ISTED *hand)*. 'Ow! That 'urt!

ISTED. Run! Run!

HACKER *grabs the handles of the cart and runs off, chased by the* SOLDIERS. *The others watch.*

STRUGGLE. He had it coming to him.

TOPLIS. There is no pleasure in the world like the spectacle of a rival stumbling. Whereas it ought to bring a shiver to your spine, should rock your bowels a little, to see what is in store for you . . .

STRUGGLE. For who?

TOPLIS. Mrs Struggle, I could see your back stripped bare if I looked in the future hard enough. I could see you held upside down and your cunt shaken to get the coins out of it. Milky coins you never even earned.

STRUGGLE. I earned. I took three hundred soldiers inside me, in a single day, before the last offensive. I had more of their confessions than a priest, and looked less bored by it. I did service. Such service I should have taken medals from the king.

TOPLIS. They also serve who only lie and act.

STRUGGLE. I was a patriot! And more than a patriot. Every groan I uttered was for them.

She leaves with KNOTTING. TRELLIS *remains, watches him.*

TOPLIS. I am the only one who came here willing it. Who wanted to be here above all other places, who was not lured here like you, or starved here like Hacker, or whipped here like the troops. *(He sits on the ground opposite her)* I used to sleep in beds soft enough for mutilated skins, the sea breeze swirling luscious curtains, the shouts of gamblers, girls' squeals, the hooting of Bugattis climbing up the midnight air, all the pinging of the Riviera beneath the snoring of a woman with her precious painted lips all wide . . . *(he looks at her)* I used to lie there knowing I should be here. Eventually, could not be anywhere but here . . . (TRELLIS *stares at him.* ERICA *enters)*

ERICA. Ah, you've found her as well! Don't tell me she's your best friend, too! Best friends are very hard to come by! I got there first! (TRELLIS *looks nervously at her)* Well, didn't I? Really, you can't mess about like this!

One minute, you're pouring out your feelings to him, and the next you're baring you soul to me! It won't do, will it? (*She pretends to hear* TRELLIS *speak*) Can I say something? Will you let me get a word in here? I—I—but—now— (*she turns mockingly to* TOPLIS) What can you do? She does go on so, I—(TRELLIS *runs off*. ERICA *watches her. Pause*) She makes me squirm. The way she suffers. Eyes fixed on the ground like that. I can't bear saints, they make me cruel. (*Pause. She walks a little way*) I have been thinking endlessly about you. (*Pause*) Endlessly. (*Pause*) Did you hear? (*Pause*) I have been expecting you to come for me, and blow me down, you haven't . (*Pause*) I must say I'm not used to this. (*Pause. She turns on him*) Christ, am I the only person with the gift of speech round here?

TOPLIS.   You are very tense.

ERICA.   Oh, come on! I did not flash my poor old tits just to get that strangled little cliché spat at me. (*He looks at her*) All right, I am tense. (*She goes to him*) Look, I'll discuss my problems and you can run your fingers up and down my hand. Will that help? (*Pause*) I am not prepared to accept that you don't fancy me.

TOPLIS.   There is such a thing as tactics. Marching towards the enemy with drums and pipes is considered clumsy nowadays . . .

ERICA.   I'd blush if I could, but something's happened to my cheeks. So many rather brutal chins. (*He looks at her*) Why do you want to humiliate me?

Sound of jeering offstage. She walks quickly away. TOPLIS *jumps to his feet as* DITCH *and* ISTED *enter, throwing their sun helmets in the air.*

TOPLIS.   My khaki loves! Show me a joy like the joy of disobedience! No woman's flickering tongue can touch it, can it, for sheer loveliness! (*They whoop gleefully*) What happened to the undertaker?

ISTED.   Gone into the matchstick trade.

TOPLIS.   Good. The officers can rot in blankets just like us. But watch him. He is all for charges, actions and the legal toffee they wrap their malice in.

ISTED.   Bayonet the bugger.

TOPLIS.   I never rule out anything.

DOWNCHILD.   Tell us about the New England. Where there are no sergeants and no drill. And the grass looks like water waving in a wind . . .

ISTED.   Shall we 'ave nigger servants? I 'ave a brother out in India says they wash the sahib's things.

TOPLIS.   Questions! Questions! The grease on the axle of progress!

ISTED.   My nigger servant, though?

TOPLIS (*taking* ISTED's *shoulders*). But answers! Answers are strained, like cacking through a sieve . . .

ISTED.   No servants, then?

TOPLIS.   Ask for the impossible. Only the impossible is worth having.

DITCH.   I don't want the impossible. I want some grass.

TOPLIS.   Grass?

ISTED.   Grass *is* impossible. Grass wants water.

DITCH (*to* TOPLIS).   Tell us we can 'ave some grass!

DOWNCHILD. Grass is 'is obsession. 'is uncle took 'im to the country once.

TOPLIS. We will have grass.

ISTED. 'ow will we? It's too bloody 'ot!

DOWNCHILD. 'e'll magic it! Won't yer, Toplis? Get some fuckin' lawn out of an 'at!

TOPLIS. Magic is setting free your dreams. No one is free unless his dreams can breathe. They blunt us with half-lives, they crush our fantasy, fill our brains with dull hopes and lowly expectations, chain us with the cheap and thrill us with the dirty. Kick off the dream-killers! Shout out your dreams!

ISTED (laughing). GRASS! GRASS! GRASS!

TOPLIS. The water at present consumed in the officers' mess, to bathe their feet and mix their whisky with, that quantity, for watering a model meadow, I hereby dedicate to Ditch! (Cheers and laughter. MUSIC enters, looks at them coldly)

MUSIC. You 'ave ripped off your flashes. You look like the starving shitters of the Siege of Kut.

ISTED. Fuck flashes! And fuck your bonny belt, it hurts my eyes.

MUSIC. I 'ave just done six days in the nick, and I emerge to see the Gallic War is lying in the latrine ditch. What's the classic now, we're studying? (He looks at TOPLIS) They tell me there is a liquor on the market known as Vino Topliso. Most lethal piss. Makes slops grow muscles and tip over carts. (Pause) I just 'elped a bloke reload 'is coffins. 'e was weeping. Someone 'ad flung sand into 'is eyes.

DOWNCHILD. We are making a new England 'ere, Eddie. From scratch. We are inventin' it.

MUSIC. You would 'ave to. There's not so much as a sparrow 'ere.

TOPLIS. I saw you once strike matches, one after another, trying to set your uniform alight. Only the rain in Flanders doused the flames. Rain is no problem here . . .

MUSIC (looking at his uniform). I like it now . . . look at that crease . . . you could draw blood with it . . .

TOPLIS. It's a brand. They could have stamped slave on your forehead just as well.

MUSIC. I will tell you what this means to me, shall I? My blinding buckle and my gorgeous crease? I stopped in Cairo once, and swaggered down a ponging street. My boots, my glisteners catching sun, did not let up their swinging, so they tumbled to avoid me, cursing one another wopwise in their haste. I am nothing if others do not shift for me. I TAKE UP SPACE. (Pause) These shogs will have no space. Ditch here looked shifty in the casbah even with a rifle. (He feints at DITCH, who moves) I claim your space! (He smiles at TOPLIS) You see?

TOPLIS. Eddie, I will have you with me.

MUSIC. Who needs me when you have this clot of acolytes? (He nuts towards DITCH, who winces again) I SAID ACOLYTES! Look, they are afraid I'll nut 'em. What lovely acolytes! Do you know acolyte, Private Ditch? The meaning of? No? Acolyte is a limpet, a nasty sort of cockle that sticks to flesh and sucks through slimy hooks. (TOPLIS laughs) Well, what is it, then? (TOPLIS *places his hands on* MUSIC'S *shoulders*) I would not let you do that if I had not loved you once.

TOPLIS.   This is my empire. Join my empire. I have come for you.

MUSIC (*looking at* TOPLIS' *hands*).   Your hands are lovely as a desk clerk's in a feather factory. I'd watch those hands. Blokes will be laying their cocks in 'em. *(He turns to go)*

TOPLIS.   Eddie. *(He stops)* You told me once you only knew one happy day. The day we stripped the general at Etaples and used his baton on his balls. 'Such distinguished bollocks,' I quote one Sergeant Music, 'should be served on silver. Where is the hallmarked bollock tray?' Such an oration on the old man's dangling apparatus to make the whole battallion rock, a joy to wipe four years of war away. We are only happy when we're free, and only free when we resist. I loathe a slogan, but you know it's true. *(Pause)*

MUSIC.   I do resist. I resist you. *(He goes out. They watch him depart)*

TOPLIS.   You could take some men to the gates of Heaven and say run riot in there, leap over tinkling streams and jump the maidens, stuff yourself on fruits the like of which you've never seen, and they would still hang back, and pick their noses, snot-chewing and dirty finger-nailed . . . *(Pause)*

Scene Five

The office in Government House. PORCELAIN *is typing.* PAIN *is on the telephone.*

PAIN.   Winston? T.E. *(Pause)* You are in bed. *(Pause)* My lion sleeps. *(Pause)* I said—*(Pause)* No, I did not ring about my book! I swear not! *(Pause)* Thank you. Thank you. From the bottom of my vain little pigeon's heart? *(Pause)* My vain pigeon's heart, I said—*(Pause, excitedly, laughing)* No. I don't! I don't know what the title means! *(He giggles)* I don't, I don't! I just liked it. I could have said Eight Pillars, I suppose! Or nine! *(Pause)* Oh, my little pigeon heart goes flutter, flutter, what—*(Pause)* 'Each page a plunge into a bath of mighty thought.' Thank you. Thank you. Our prose is twinned. Our prose is out of the same bloody English womb—*(Pause)* Womb. *(Pause)* WOMB! *(Pause)* Oh, listen, genius . . . *(Pause)* I die here. I perish of triviality. I bleed of it, but listen— *(Pause)* You must send specialists. Our sore homesick English crack. Yes. Crack.

There is a commotion outside. HACKER *shoves his way in.*

HACKER.   I am not movin'! I have lost stock and I want compensation!

PORCELAIN.   Please don't shout . . .

HACKER.   I will shout! I see no alternative in shouting! SHOW ME AN ALTERNATIVE AND I WILL DO IT.

PORCELAIN.   I am not part of the government. I am just using the typewriter.

HACKER.   WHAT IS GOING ON 'ERE, PAIN?

PAIN.   *(putting the receiver down).*   An epidemic.

HACKER. Correction. Two epidemics. One caused by amoebic amoebas and the other by stroppy buggers. And nothing being done about it.

PAIN *(going out)*. They have sprayed the barracks, I understand.

HACKER. WELL, SPRAY THE FUCKING OCCUPANTS!

ERICA *(entering in a dressing-gown)*. What is all the noise about?

HACKER. Oh, she comes, fresh from 'er bed! IT IS MIDDAY, MISS!

ERICA *(Taking the seat proffered by* PORCELAIN). Thank you, I will sit there. I seem to wake up tireder than I go to bed.

HACKER. I 'ave to tell you this, the business community is seething.

ERICA. Community?

HACKER. I AM SEETHING!

ERICA. Ronald, would you bring me a cup of tea? And an asprin? (PORCELAIN *goes out*)

HACKER. The conditions necessary for the conduct of good business are as follows; one, ample profits. Two, ample police. There is neither police nor profits. I 'ope I am not shouting . Please tell me if I do BUT THEY NEARLY MURDERED ME.

ERICA. The Governor lies in on Thursdays.

HACKER. The Governor is gaga. You make the decisions 'ere.

ERICA. I dream of sleep. That is not such a paradox as it appears. (PORCELAIN *returns*) In my dream I am a crusader. Solid marble, on a slab, deep in a vault where no sound penetrates. Conditions are ideal, but I'm restless.

PORCELAIN. Someone is carving their initials on your feet?

ERICA. I want to scream, but being marble, cannot. I am so full of terror I wake up.

HACKER. Can I borrow a telephone?

ERICA. Why?

HACKER. I want to lodge a complaint.

ERICA. With whom?

HACKER. Churchill.

ERICA. Put it in writing.

HACKER. I can't.

ERICA. Can't write?

HACKER. CHRIST, I CAME 'ERE FOR PROTECTION! I CAME 'ERE WITH A BROKEN 'EAD!

ERICA. Yes . . .

HACKER *(turning away)*. Excuse me, I can see your breasts . . . *(She covers herself, gets up, walks away a little, her back turned to him)* I thought the law was made for citizens. I am educated. What's 'alf a pint of blood to buy a bit of truth like that? *(He goes out.* PORCELAIN *carries on typing with two fingers)*

ERICA. I cannot say I'm happy here. I don't think I have ever known real happiness, have you?

PORCELAIN. Yes.

ERICA. What's it like?

PORCELAIN *(stops typing)*. It's—

ERICA.   No, don't tell me! *(She smiles)* You're going to say it's something
very small and beautiful, aren't you? Something that came over you while
standing in the tube? Sunlight on a window? A skylark singing when the
shelling stopped? *(Pause)*

PORCELAIN.   Sitting with my mother having tea.

ERICA.   Quite. I don't think it's happiness I want. It's ecstasy.

PORCELAIN.   That was ecstasy.

ERICA.   Ecstasy?

PORCELAIN.   My mother's died, you see. *(He looks at her)*

ERICA.   Died? *(He nods, gravely)* And is that very, very terrible? I ask
because I had no mother.

PORCELAIN.   Yes. **(***Pause***)**

ERICA.   I'm sorry. If I'd known I would have dressed. *(She pulls her gown
tighter round her)* No. That's silly. You don't want me to be hypocritical, do
you? You don't want me to be sympathetic when I'm not, do you? *(He
shakes his head. He is weeping)* You do! Oh, you do! *(She goes, cradles his
head)* May I tell you something very terrible? *(He snorts)* You see, I am
more conscious at this moment of being in love than of your mother dying.
Overwhelmingly more interested in that trivial little fact, that dirty little
wanting, than all the dying mothers in the universe. Are you listening? *(He
snorts)* I could go further, shall I? *(He snorts)* I could say, if I could have
him, just have him once, or bring your mother back, I would choose, I
know I would, to—*(He shudders in her arms)* I know . . . ! I know how vile
that is! I do think human beings are CONTEMPTIBLE, don't you? *(She
starts to cry as well. They hold one another)* Can you bear my honesty? *(He
snorts favourably)* Oh, good! Oh, good! I do like you!

TALLBOY *rushes into the room with a pistol.*

TALLBOY.   There is the spy! There is the spy!

ERICA.   What are you—*(She screams as* TALLBOY *shoots* PORCELAIN
through the head)

TALLBOY.   THE SPY IS DEAD! THE SPY IS DEAD! WHAT ARE
YER WEEPING FOR? THE SPY IS DEAD!

ACT TWO

Scene One

PAIN *is sitting cross-legged outside a tent.*

PAIN.   English soldiers bathing in the Sea of Galilee. *(Pause)*
I drew to me the slander in their voices,
Shy in nakedness their village accents hung like smoke in air,
White-limbed and picking over stones like girls on beaches,
My blood stood still in wonder at my brothers there . . .
(Pause. MUSIC *emerges from the tent, looks at* PAIN, *long and hard)*
Good? Was it?

MUSIC.   I kissed 'er bum like it was the only bum to wobble under skirt. I shoved 'er. And when I came off, she was pig flesh, spotty and raw with rash. But that's the way of it. You will 'ave noticed, sitting there, the ocean of change in our expressions, before and after. WHY DO YOU SIT THERE?

PAIN.   Why not?

MUSIC.   I RESENT IT.

PAIN.   I make you feel ashamed. Don't be ashamed. For me.

MUSIC.   You are so little, and so clean . . .

PAIN.   I discovered once the power of abstention. The authority of not. Not made me a leader. Because men will follow him who does not, out of respect for his will . . . (PAIN *looks at him, goes out.* KNOTTING *appears from the tent, looking for a customer)* Nobody else, I'm afraid. Typhus has seduced your favourites away.

KNOTTING.   You are my favourite.

PAIN.   Ah. I was afraid you might say that.

KNOTTING.   Come in.

PAIN.   Thank you, no.

KNOTTING.   Why not?

PAIN.   Why not? Why not is such a pitiful reason for doing anything. I like why better.

KNOTTING.   All right. Because it is the greatest beauty in the world. Poets say so. No one can match our testimonials.

PAIN.   That's love, isn't it? They are referring to? I think?

KNOTTING.   This is love, Mr Lawrence.

PAIN.   No, I am not Mr Lawrence, and this is not love, it's sex.

KNOTTING.   Only to begin with. At the doorway, it is sex. In a few minutes. I promise you, it will be love. Love without the conversation.

PAIN.   I'm trying to write a poem.

KNOTTING *(kneeling beside him).*   I'll just touch you, shall I?

PAIN.   No, I don't like to be touched.

KNOTTING.   I have the best fingers in the business. Shut your eyes.

PAIN.   Listen, I am reluctant to offend you, but I don't like women. In this way. Or in any other, very much . . .

KNOTTING. Couldn't you just lie there?

PAIN. For whom?

KNOTTING. For me. *(Pause)* I know who you are. You are Lawrence of Arabia. I gave you my drawers at Catterick.

PAIN. I have never been in Catterick.

KNOTTING. It's all right, you're safe with me.

PAIN. You are making a terrible mistake.

KNOTTING. I am sick of squaddies. I am sick of squaddie spunk and squaddie sentiments. What wouldn't I give to 'ear some decent words, some love in proper English.

PAIN. Perhaps you're in the wrong profession? I dare suggest, in the heat of the moment, Einstein's vocabulary is scarcely different from a corporal's in the Lancs. I may be wrong.

KNOTTING. You thing . . . you bint . . . you bag . . . etcetera . . .

PAIN. Quite.

KNOTTING. Vile.

PAIN. Is it?

KNOTTING. You wouldn't say that.

PAIN. Well, I don't know.

KNOTTING. No. Not you . . .

PAIN. I feel sure I would be . . . just as commonplace as that . . .

KNOTTING. Try.

PAIN. I don't think so—

KNOTTING *(grasping his hand)*. Just try!

PAIN. Let go of me.

KNOTTING. It's only flesh . . . !

PAIN. LET GO OF ME. *(Pause. She releases his hand)* You have no idea how easy it would be for me to be unkind to you. So terribly unkind to you. And I don't wish to be . . .

A SOLDIER *walks smartly on stage, holding a declaration. He is followed by a* BOY SOLDIER *holding boxes. The elder of the two stands on a box.*

OLD. BY ORDER! BY ORD–ER OF THE GOV–ERNOR! SALE OF EFFECTS OF THE DECEASED! VIZ, SHIRTS SILK, NEW, SEVENTEEN! *(As he lists the items, the* SOLDIERS, TOPLIS, HACKER, STRUGGLE, TRELLIS *and* MUSIC *form a crowd about him)* SOCKS, COTTON, NEW, PAIRS, TWENTY-THREE, UNDERPANTS, SHORT, FIVE, LONG, FIVE, PAIRS, NEW, HAIR BRUSH AND COMB, SILK HANDKERCHIEFS, COD LIVER OIL AND LIFE-SIZED DOLL, FOREMENTIONED ITEMS TO BE AUCTIONED AND WITHOUT RESERVE! John, thank you. *(He passes him the paper)* Lot one is shirts, unworn, with the maker's label in the neck, the label reading LILLYWHITE OF BOND STREET, and the size, John, please?

YOUNG. Fifteen.

OLD. Come again?

YOUNG. Fifteen.

OLD. Neck fifteen, quantity, seventeen. I open bidding at TWO BOB A SHIRT!

ISTED. 'ow much?

OLD. TWO BOB A SHIRT! Show 'em, John, please—'old the fucking thing out, son, let the sunlight catch it—pure silk that is, softer than a—

TOPLIS. Tuppence.

OLD. 'ullo, the wits 'ave got among us. At two bob a shirt, then, two bob only, feel it, John, will yer, John will up'old me, it slips through yer fingers like the minge of a mandarin's mistress—

TOPLIS. All right, a penny, then. (*The* SOLDIERS *laugh*)

OLD. I make the jokes 'ere, son, all right? In gorgeous cream, or mushroom, is it?

YOUNG. Mushroom.

OLD. John says mushroom, I say cream, but never mind the shade. I'm starting, not at five bob, not at four, no, not at three bob either, but—

TOPLIS. Why doesn't he listen to me? I said a penny, didn't I?

OLD (*catching* STRUGGLE'S *eye*). Two bob! Thank you, I 'ave a start!

TOPLIS. I wonder if the auctioneer is deaf?

OLD (*at a nod from* HACKER). And two-and-six! And two-and-six!

TOPLIS. Can you hear me on your box?

OLD. Three shillings! Thank you, Madam, someone who knows the difference between price and value!

TOPLIS (*waving his hand under* OLD'S *nose*). Hello?

OLD. Come on, now, these are dirt cheap, these are under cost price, way under cost price, I don't think I can let these go—

TOPLIS. All right! A HALFPENNY, then!

OLD. 'ow long 'ave we been 'ere, 'ow long 'ave we been 'ere, John?

ISTED. TOO FUCKING LONG!

OLD. Too dash-dash long, the man says, and 'ave we ever clapped our eyes on stuff like this, I ask you, 'ave we ever—THREE-AND-SIX!

TOPLIS. I have made my offer and I want the shirts. Will you be so good as to hand me the shirts?

DOWNCHILD. Give 'im the shirts!

OLD. At three-and-six, then, at three-and-six these cream silk shirts—(*He looks rounds, claps his hands*) The gentleman at the back! John, thank you.

TOPLIS. I am not at the back. I am at the front.

OLD. Thank you, John, and the next lot is—what is the next lot?

TOPLIS. You are deaf and short-sighted. You have forfeited your right to be an auctioneer. A new auctioneer, please! This man is incompetent!

YOUNG (*lifting up a pair*). Pants.

OLD. Gents' pants! Pants long and short, in matching cream or mushroom silk, the label in the back says—what does it say, John?

YOUNG. Lily—

OLD. LILYWHITE OF BOND STREET, thank you, 'old 'em out, son, 'old 'em out for fuck's sake, let the people see—

TOPLIS (*snatching the pants*). Oh, hear them whisper as you draw them up your hairy rump! Hear the label talking! No perfumed mistress will fear to let her knickers fall in company with these! So throw off your army issue, chuck your chaffers in the ditch and prance in these!

OLD.　Thank you, I could not 'ave put it better myself. One shilling, then? One shilling, please! (HACKER *nods*) One shilling! Over there!

TOPLIS *(pulling them over his shorts)*.　Oh, am I not lovely now? Do I not command the sprawl of lovely women when I parade in these?

OLD *(as* STRUGGLE *nods)*.　One-and-sixpence! One-and-sixpence and I throw in that pair for free—

MUSIC.　I bid—I bid I only break your nose.

OLD.　Two shillings! Two shillings! (STRUGGLE *nods again*) Two-and-sixpence!

HACKER *(to* STRUGGLE).　Come on, woman, for Jesus' blood and guts, don't bid against me, eh?

MUSIC.　Not a broken head—not a broken jaw—not a busted liver—I only break your nose.

OLD *(responding to* HACKER'S *nod)*.　Three shillings, thank you—

MUSIC *(walking to* OLD).　Your nose.

OLD.　Eddie—

MUSIC.　YOUR NOSE, I SAID. *(Pause)*

OLD.　I think, in the interests of—in everybody's interest—I am suspending business. Pack the stuff away, John, please.

PAIN.　The doll. (OLD *climbs off the box*) You have not sold the doll.

OLD.　John, please—

MUSIC.　THE DOLL, 'E SAID. *(Pause.* OLD *looks around him)*

OLD.　Unpack the doll. (YOUNG *looks confused*) Come on, son! (YOUNG *unpacks a large, fussily-dressed doll)*

PAIN.　Would you be kind enough to start the bidding?

OLD.　Yes . . . well . . . er . . .

ISTED.　Sell it!

OLD.　I'm trying to! *(Pause)* This is a most—uncommon item—a female doll—right, John, a female doll?

YOUNG.　Female.

OLD.　Female, definitely . . . and . . . er . . . I dunno what to ask for this . . . a bob?

PAIN.　I take it.

OLD.　Thank you. Give it to 'im, and let's shove off. (YOUNG *goes to give the doll to* PAIN)

TOPLIS.　Isn't this an auction? I thought it was an auction. I have only heard one bid.

OLD.　Well, is there any other?

TOPLIS.　I bid.

OLD.　You bid . . . (MUSIC *grins*) I 'ave a bid. *(Pause)* One shilling and sixpence. (PAIN *nods*) Two bob. (TOPLIS) And six. (PAIN) Three bob. (TOPLIS) And six. (PAIN) And four. (TOPLIS) And five.

PAIN.　This man has not got five shillings.

TOPLIS.　This man has no need of a doll.

OLD.　Gents, I am only 'ere to do a job—

TOPLIS.　The doll is rotten with old England! Look at it! Lift up its skirts, out comes a stink! Squeeze its belly, oh, the pong of death!

PAIN.　The doll stood for his mother . . .

TOPLIS *(prodding it).* It's stiff from squatting over tea tables, dumb from muttering contempt! We bled here while it fussed and farted. A bayonet, please, I will put it out its misery!

PAIN. It was his mother . . .

TOPLIS. I STAND IN THE GREATEST CONTEMPT OF MOTHERS!

STRUGGLE. Only because you can't find one who will acknowledge you.

TOPLIS. All religions I stamp on! And mother worship with my stiffest boots! Show me a mother who refused the government her son. Did yours? Did yours? No, none. They wept instead, and by their weeping, washed all the guilt away.

PAIN. This is a very wordy juggler, better with vocabulary than coloured balls, but words are so much easier to keep in the air . . .

TOPLIS. I execute the doll! Someone lend me a bayonet! *(He looks at them. No one moves)*

OLD. That doll is government property.

TOPLIS. I murder government! In Flanders I stood on a canal embankment and toppled generals down the slope! I set the camp alive like ants kicked out their nest, winged and scurrying with indignation! I lifted up the souls of men bent double in the beckoning of futile death! This man is my witness, I never shrunk from government! (MUSIC *draws his bayonet from its scabbard)*

PAIN. It is a harmless bag of wool. Why all the rhetoric? He kissed it when he went to bed.

STRUGGLE. He's scared of it. Toplis is frightened of a doll.

TOPLIS. IT IS NO DOLL! *(Pause.* PAIN *smiles)*

PAIN. Not a doll? It is a doll. I can confirm it is a doll. (STRUGGLE *grins.* PAIN *invites* ISTED *forward)* Examine it, will you? Take its pulse?

HACKER. Toplis is mad

PAIN. I cannot find its pulse. Or heartbeat. Does it breathe?

HACKER. Toplis, you daft bugger . . .

PAIN. I am no anatomist, but I can confirm it has no bones. No, this is not living tissue. *(He cups his ear to its chest)* Anyone inside there? Hello? Hello? *(Some laughter. Suddenly* TRELLIS *steps forward)*

TRELLIS. IT AIN'T A DOLL. *(They look at her)* Yer love a doll, don't yer? 'ow could anyone love that? *(Pause)* It ain't a doll. It's what walks along the pavement with two pissin' dogs. It's what 'ates children. *(She looks at* MUSIC) Stab it or I will.

STRUGGLE. Sandra, you are not well, dear.

(YOUNG *and* OLD *try to slip away. She spots then)*

TRELLIS. Don't run away! You ain't the enemy! *(They stop)* Because you flog the stuff, don't mean you 'ave ter lick it.

STRUGGLE. Go to your tent and lie down.

DITCH. Lie down yourself! (KNOTTING *bursts out laughing)*

TRELLIS *(to* MUSIC). Are yer doing it? *(He looks at her)* All right, I will! *(She takes the bayonet off him and thrusts it in the doll)*

TOPLIS. Oh, let your madness out! Your just, clean madness, let it out! Or it will blow your heart away!

ISTED *(Rushing up and stabbing it).* No blood!

TRELLIS. What did yer expect!

DITCH *(rushing to the boxes).* Silk shirts! Silk pants! *(With a cheer, they rush to seize the goods)*

DOWNCHILD. My drawers! My mushroom knickers, give 'em 'ere!

ISTED. Share 'em out!

TOPLIS. Oh, dance you robbers! Dance! *(There is a whooping)*

MUSIC. Get to the armoury, you silly bleeders . . .

DOWNCHILD *(to* DITCH). Oi! Give that 'ere! (DITCH *is filling his arms*) My silk drawers, you!

MUSIC. Fuck your drawers! Get to the armoury!

TRELLIS. *(They stop.* TRELLIS *sees* HACKER *attempting to slip away*) Where are yer going, Hacker?

HACKER. Left the kettle on. Where do you think?

TOPLIS. Tell them we've moved! Tell them hold the weapons, quick! (ISTED *runs off, holding shirts and bayonet*) Go with him! Quick! (DITCH *runs off*)

PAIN. They will bomb you from aeroplanes. Like naughty Arabs, they will burn your tents . . .

TOPLIS. No. We will fly our flag at them, and they will put their wheels down, and give us their goggles and their gloves.

PAIN. Your flag? What flag is that? There is only one flag. The jack. The rag of your race.

TRELLIS. We 'ave a flag!

PAIN *(turning).* You have? What is a mutineer's flag, do tell me. The symbol of mischief on a ground of black?

TRELLIS. This. *(She unhitches her skirt)* Fly this. *(She tosses it to* TOPLIS)

TOPLIS. It's a warm flag . . . it has not fluttered over any poor dim conscript's blood . . . (PAIN *turns to go*)

MUSIC. Kiss it. *(He stops)* No one departs without 'e kisses it.

TOPLIS *(from the bottom of his heart).* Oh, Eddie, remember when you last said that? Of a dead private's helmet, bullet-riddled like a sieve? The Major-General crouched and put his lips to it . . .

MUSIC. Then scuttled to 'is office and called down artillery . . . *(He still looks at* PAIN) Pay it respect. *(He does not move)*

TRELLIS. Join.

PAIN. I join nothing. I never have.

MUSIC. Oh, come on, you cold and shrivelled little man!

PAIN. I'm not free, then?

MUSIC. Free to kiss it.

PAIN. But not free not to? Freedom is not, is it not?

TRELLIS. No!

PAIN. What is it, then?

TRELLIS. It's sticking by yer mates.

MUSIC. I will 'ave you kiss it. Private Pain.

PAIN. Please, don't try to break my will. Can't you see a free will without wanting to break it?

MUSIC (*pushing the point of the bayonet on* PAIN'S *neck*). Kiss it. (PAIN
edges slowly forward) Oh, look at 'im, 'is lips would rubber out a thousand
feet to keep 'im from the spunk stains of 'is friends . . . *(His lips touch it. He
falls onto his hands)*
KNOTTING.   'e ain't Lawrence. 'e ain't Lawrence after all.
TOPLIS (*to* DOWNCHILD).   Arrest the officers! And lock them in a small
room, they will confess one another to death. (DOWNCHILD *and*
TRELLIS *go out.* TOPLIS *looks at* KNOTTING) Go with her. Your
mouth would win the waverers to any cause.
KNOTTING.   Sorry. I'm a patriot.
TOPLIS.   Good, I love a patriot. Put on your brightest skirt.

She goes out. HACKER *and* STRUGGLE *come quickly forward, kiss the
skirt, go out.* MUSIC *looks at* TOPLIS.

MUSIC.   I don't think you are what you were . . .
TOPLIS.   I'm not?
MUSIC.   I watched you, and you 'ad to struggle.
TOPLIS.   Did I?
MUSIC.   Something's gone. Only the tart saved you, you could not 'ave
saved yerself. The words were stiffer than the 'inges on a pillbox door.
TOPLIS.   Even so, you joined.
MUSIC.   To spare their pain a little bit. When they lie kickin' under sticks
and boots. What will you tell those shrimps when wall-eyed sergeants bust
their lips?
TOPLIS.   How beautiful they were. How they were very briefly gods . . .
(TOPLIS *looks at him, appalled*)
MUSIC.   Oh, you little dribble, what 'ave you done . . . ?

He goes out.

Scene Two

The Governor's House. ERICA *is lying on a sofa,* TALLBOY *sitting in his
wheelchair. A clock chimes.*

TALLBOY.   Why do you sit here? Go to bed.
ERICA.   Shh! *(She sits forward, listens, sinks back)*
TALLBOY.   You've never looked young. Even as a girl, particularly
joyless—
ERICA.   Shh! *(She sits up again)*
TALLBOY.   And potato-skinned. No sheen on you, or sparkle-eyed. A
woman has to sleep.
ERICA.   I do not ask you to sit up with me, do I? How can I hear him if he
comes?
TALLBOY.   Won't come.
ERICA.   Shut up.
TALLBOY.   For your old tissue, will he? I would not. *(Pause)* Have you
made out the report on the spy?

ERICA.　Yes.

TALLBOY.　Saying he slipped down a ravine?

ERICA.　There are no ravines here.

TALLBOY.　There's no water, either. He arrived on a lie, let him go on one.

ERICA.　It scarcely matters, does it? As we don't govern any more. I can't think why they haven't shot us. I hate to be ignored.

TALLBOY.　It is the essence of happiness. My lovely stroke. My gorgeous clot. You cannot know the joy that comes of giving up all serious attempts at communication. If you died, I shouldn't blink.

ERICA.　We can't both simulate strokes. It's too much of a coincidence.

TALLBOY.　The spectacle, from here, of your persistent itch, like streptococchi squirming on a culture dish—

ERICA.　Look, you are very voluble for a vegetable! I am a simple girl and I want to get married!

TALLBOY.　Gibberish.

ERICA.　Just go to bed! (*Pause. He turns and wheels himself from the room. ERICA walks up and down*) He's afraid of me. For one of two reasons. He loves me, or he hates me. That's the problem with sex. The same behaviour is consistent with desire or repulsion. The same expression in the face. I've often expected to be murdered and been fucked. Some poor strangled girl must have experienced the opposite, I expect. But all passion is a risk— WHAT'S THAT! (*She freezes. TOPLIS is standing in the door. Pause. She closes her eyes*)

TOPLIS.　I am running out of words. I am running out of magic.

ERICA.　Yes.

TOPLIS.　I find myself—in the midst of conjuring—I find myself—thinking of you.

ERICA.　Me.

TOPLIS.　Undressed.

ERICA.　Yes.

TOPLIS.　It breaks the spell you see. To think of women. Just as when you are with a woman it breaks the spell to think of anything else.

ERICA.　Yes.

TOPLIS.　It is very hard to teach magic. To men who are dull. When you are thinking, she will have me if I go to her.

ERICA.　Is it.

TOPLIS.　Yes.

ERICA.　Well, then.

TOPLIS.　Can I?

ERICA.　Yes. Rather roughly. Rather indelicately.

TOPLIS.　Yes.

ERICA.　As if you were mad. Please. So I know that I exist? So that I know through all the chatter and the stale grey slime of this I am somebody's agony! Make me feel your pain.

She turns to him. Blackout.

Scene Three

The desert. A roar of aircraft engines. TWO MEN *in sun helmets duck as if under wings, shirts flapping in the airstream. They watch the plane take off, the sound recedes.*

SLIPPER.   Lovely, lovely, RAF . . .
CASHIN *(waving).*   Bye bye . . . bye bye . . .

Pause. SLIPPER *shakes out a map. He looks at it, turns to* CASHIN.

SLIPPER.   I have a hard on. I have a great big thing here.
CASHIN.   Dublin.
SLIPPER.   Just like Dublin. My horn. My killing stick.
CASHIN.   Yes.
SLIPPER.   Can I tell you something? Can I tell you I love this? Can I say that I feel such a power in me I could—don't be offended—on the ground here have you—though I'm not one bit homo, do you follow? I am so thrilled, I think it is?
CASHIN.   I don't want—
SLIPPER.   No, but, say you understand it, please?
CASHIN.   I see it as a job—
SLIPPER.   More than a job—
CASHIN.   A task—
SLIPPER.   A passion, though? To be at the end of all that English business, to be the biting bit, the last hard needle of that desk and thick carpet Whitehall stuff, the corridors and papers, parliamentary Autumn leaves and pretty London democratic Big Ben thing? To actually kill? I am so big . . .
VASHIN.   Yes.
SLIPPER.   To be unmerciful. The sheer perfection of being unmerciful. Say you understand me, please?
CASHIN.   I think I know.
SLIPPER.   Must know it, Don. Or make me feel some freak.
CASHIN.   No, no . . . (SLIPPER *looks at him*)
SLIPPER.   We go directly East . . .

They go out.

Scene Four

A flagpole with the skirt attached. Kneeling with a watering can, DITCH. *He tends invisible grass seed with exquisite care. After a few moments,* MUSIC *and* DOWNCHILD *pass through, carrying a folded stretcher.*

DITCH.   MIND MY SEED! (*They stop.* MUSIC *looks down*)
MUSIC.   What seed?
DITCH.   There.
MUSIC.   Where?

DITCH. Just mind it.
MUSIC. Can't see it.
DITCH. STANDING IN IT!
MUSIC *(stepping back)*. Where?
DITCH. AND THERE! *(He starts brushing the soil)* Oh, Jesus Christ . . .
MUSIC (*watching* DITCH *from a distance*).   Ain't no seed. (*He looks to*
    DOWNCHILD) No seed is there?
DITCH *(cruelly)*.   BLIND GIT.

MUSIC *shrugs. They go out.* DITCH *returns to his labours. Sound of voices
off.* TRELLIS, KNOTTING, STRUGGLE *and* ERICA *enter, skipping and
passing footballs.*

TRELLIS. Start! Erica!
ERICA. Me?
TRELLIS. Yes! Start! Quick!
DITCH. Er—
ERICA. The New Englishwoman—
STRUGGLE. Relishes—
KNOTTING. Her life—
ERICA. She is—
TRELLIS. Nimble—
DITCH. Er—
STRUGGLE. Smart—
KNOTTING. Intelligent—
DITCH. MY FUCKING GRASS.
ERICA. She—(ERICA *misses the ball. Pause*)
DITCH. You're on my grass.

They look at him. He points to the ground. The WOMEN *move back a few feet
in each direction. He goes back to watering and tending.*

ERICA. She—
TRELLIS. Examines—
STRUGGLE. Her mind—
KNOTTING. Her conscience—
ERICA. Her vagina—
TRELLIS. She is—
STRUGGLE. Critical—
KNOTTING. Creative—
ERICA. Co-operative—*(She misses the ball, closes her eyes in dismay)*
TRELLIS. Erica . . .
ERICA. No.
TRELLIS. Please. You're spoiling it for the rest of us. (*Pause, then* ERICA
    kneels)
ERICA. The desert is green. The desert is green. The desert is green. *(She
    jumps up)*
TRELLIS (*to* KNOTTING, *who has the ball*).   Jane.
ERICA. Really, this is so much—
TRELLIS. Don't just criticize. Anyone can criticize. Suggest something.

KNOTTING. I got a suggestion. We all go 'ome.

TRELLIS. No, we don't! We don't go 'ome! This is our 'ome! Where do you wanna go to?

KNOTTING. Joking.

TRELLIS. Not funny.

KNOTTING. No.

TRELLIS. Suggest, then, Erica.

ERICA. I can't.

TRELLIS. Exactly.

ERICA. I hate it.

TRELLIS. You 'ate it.

ERICA. Yes.

TRELLIS. Go on.

ERICA. Go on?

STRUGGLE. Let's get on with the game—

TRELLIS. No. Let's 'elp Erica! (*Pause. She looks at* ERICA, *who looks at the ground*) I 'ate it, I—*(Pause)* 'ate myself?

ERICA. Well, of course I hate myself.

TRELLIS. Exactly.

ERICA. I have always hated myself.

TRELLIS. Exactly.

ERICA. I wish you would stop saying that! Exactly what, exactly?

TRELLIS. You are always on about yourself.

ERICA. Can't help it.

TRELLIS. What are you? You are just a little pebble on a great big beach—

ERICA. Quite, and I hate it.

TRELLIS. Listen! Listen! Shut yer eyes! (ERICA *closes her eyes*) Think of a storm. Think of a storm that's lasted for a million years—

ERICA. Two million—

TRELLIS. Two million years! Now think of one single, little raindrop—

ERICA. One raindrop—

TRELLIS. Then think, that little raindrop 'as a million parts—

ERICA. Two million—

TRELLIS. Two million parts. You are one of those little parts. (*Pause.* ERICA *opens her eyes*)

ERICA. I still hate it. Only more so.

TRELLIS. Got to see yerself as part of things! (MUSIC *and* DOWNCHILD *come in with a body on a stretcher*)

MUSIC. Oh, look, the jelly shiver of their bums! The rasp of skirt on knicker!

STRUGGLE. Do you have to come past here?

DITCH *(indicating)*. Grass . . .

MUSIC. Oh, give a man 'is daily throb!

DITCH. Grass . . .

KNOTTING. In the New England there ain't no filthy language, is there, Sandra?

TRELLIS. There ain't no filthy language 'cos there ain't no filthy thoughts.

MUSIC. 'o says 'is thoughts are filthy? *(He feels the blanket)* I can't feel

nothin'! The air is thick with female moisture but nothin' shifts . . .
(DOWNCHILD *laughs*) Knicker in profusion but no, he don't come up!
(DOWNCHILD *laughs*)

TRELLIS.   What's funny? Is it funny that 'e can't think of nothin' else? Is it
funny that 'e 'as to piss on us? Clear out your 'ead! Make way for
something better in your 'ead!

DITCH.   Grass . . . !

TRELLIS.   See us as comrades, will yer! Not as things to squeeze and
fuck—

MUSIC *(closing his eyes).*   When you come on like that—

TRELLIS.   As bits an' bints, as stuff an' cunt—

MUSIC.   When you come on like that—

TRELLIS.   As drippin' thing and suckin' thing—For Christ's sake share
something with us—

MUSIC.   All red-necked like that I could—DO MURDER! SEE!
*(He drops the end of the stretcher. The body lurches off.
Pause)*

DITCH.   I was diggin' there . . . I WAS DIGGIN' THERE!

TOPLIS *wanders in, watches for a moment.*

TOPLIS.   Our old comrade has slid in a heap . . . pick him up, he looks
ashamed . . .

MUSIC.   Once you could not get 'er to whisper thank you to a five pound
note.

TOPLIS.   She's free, Eddie. It's unlocked her mouth. Give her her pleasure.

MUSIC.   Pleasure? Pleasure you call that?

TOPLIS.   Thought is pleasure. Real thought. Not the thought which drips
out of professors or is strained out of a poet's bowels. Real thought.
Thought which transforms. (MUSIC *looks at him, comes close, and like a
blindman, seems to run his fingers over* TOPLIS' *face*)

MUSIC.   Where is 'e . . . I can't find 'im . . . is 'e there . . . ? *(He turns
brusquely to* DOWNCHILD) Come on! *(They heave the corpse onto the
stretcher, go out. Pause)*

KNOTTING.   I came 'ere . . . may I say this? I came 'ere to make an 'undred
quid. (TRELLIS *snorts*) Silly, ain't it? I wanted to do bed and breakfast
down in Bognor.

TOPLIS.   The tinsel in the heads of prostitutes! To look at you you'd think
the very least such lips and tossing hair would want was yachts and
dribbling lawyers. But no! It's B & B she wants, honeymooners' spotted
sheets to wash!

KNOTTING.   I can't help my face.

TOPLIS.   You help it all the time. No one has more lipsticks.

TRELLIS.   She chucked 'em in the sea! We all did!

KNOTTING.   I'm sorry, I still think old England suits me best. I try to be
nimble and smart but I don't think I'm intelligent.

TRELLIS.   You are intelligent!

KNOTTING.   Let's face it, Sandra, I'm not, darling . . .

STRUGGLE.   She's not. Are you? You are lovely but you're not intelligent.

TRELLIS *(turning angrily on her)*. Don't 'elp 'er to be ignorant!

KNOTTING. Look, the New Englishwoman is honest, isn't she?

TRELLIS. Yes.

KNOTTING. All right, I'll be honest. I miss the officers.

TRELLIS. Oh, Jesus—

KNOTTING. I do, Sandra!

TRELLIS *(to TOPLIS, desperately)*. Argue! Argue with 'er!

TOPLIS *(laughing, putting his arms round KNOTTING)*. Oh, Jane, Jane wants the fish and chips and coloured lights—

TRELLIS. Don't cuddle 'er . . .

TOPLIS. The creaking stairs smelling faintly of shit . . .

KNOTTING. Never said that—

TOPLIS. The coitus and the banging water pipes . . .

TRELLIS. ARGUE! (TOPLIS *buries his head in* KNOTTING'S *shoulder, laughs. Pause*)

STRUGGLE. Toplis has been in the sun too long . . .

TOPLIS *(turning from KNOTTING)*. It's so simple, isn't it? Scattering the farmyard ducks. Oh, the racket, oh, the din and feathers! But later, when they flock around again, and ask, where is our water, where's our grain, what good is it to say, grain and water? Why? I have transformed you! Are you still a duck?

TRELLIS. Argue. Yer find the answer in the argument. *(He looks at her)* WHERE ELSE! *(She goes out, stops, returns, calls the other women)* There is a meeting! 'urry up! (KNOTTING *and* STRUGGLE *go out. Pause*)

ERICA. Will you make me different? I am waiting to be different. Has it happened yet?

TOPLIS. Every time someone looks in our eyes, we wonder, could this be the man, the woman, who will make me different? But in the weary, yellow morning, the mirror tells us, no, if anything, you are more yourself . . .

ERICA. What are you doing here? *(Pause)* I think I could die, still waiting to be born.

TOPLIS. The cry of the garden suburbs, where the trees are pink and orange, to match the colour of the gin . . .

ERICA. And your slum, stinking of piss, sliding on bottles, tripping over whippets. Will you touch me? Tell me I destroy you. Do I? Do I, a little bit?

He goes to take her, roughly, begins to take off her clothes. CASHIN *and* SLIPPER *enter. They separate.*

SLIPPER. We're looking for Government House.

TOPLIS. You can have the Government. Or you can have the house. But not together.

SLIPPER. Where's the government?

TOPLIS. In the soldiers' heads.

CASHIN. All right, then, where's the house? (ERICA *points off*)

SLIPPER. Thank you. *(They walk off.* TOPLIS *watches them)*

TOPLIS. My executioners have arrived.

ERICA. How do you know?

TOPLIS. They are public schoolboys. Look at the flapping way they walk, as if grace were a sin, and their faces, rigid with the explusion of all doubt. In the war, when we carried them dying from their wounds, it did not slip. Only at the moment of death it cracked, and a thick slab of misery oozed out. *(Pause)* They're here to kill me. *(Pause)*

ERICA. I will kill them. Let me. Let me sin for you . . .

Fade to black.

Scene Five

The same place, in the dead of night. TWO FIGURES *move stealthily about the flagpole, from which* TRELLIS' *skirt hangs.*

HACKER. Come on, Struggle, yer clumsy bitch!

STRUGGLE. Upside down—

HACKER. What is?

STRUGGLE. Flag—

HACKER. Fuck that, just run it up—

STRUGGLE. Er—

HACKER. Now what?

STRUGGLE. Er—

HACKER. Fuck, what!

STRUGGLE. Stuck.

HACKER. Where?

STRUGGLE. On the pulley.

HACKER *(tugging the rope desperately)*. Fuckin' 'ell! Did you do this!

STRUGGLE. Shh!

HACKER. Keep a look out. I'll 'ave to get up to the top. Give us 'and up.

STRUGGLE. 'ow?

HACKER. Bend down. Go on, bend down. *(She kneels. He climbs on her back)* Sod this. *(He begins climbing the pole)* The things we do for liberty—WHASSAT! *(A torch beam reveals* HACKER *half way up the flagpole)* DON'T SHOOT! I can explain it! Don't shoot . . . *(footsteps out of the darkness, and* PAIN *appears)*

PAIN. A lovely night for propaganda. I was thinking of daubing a few walls myself . . .

HACKER. 'o is it?

PAIN. A slogan here, a slogan there, breaking out like sores on lips. To greet the New English as they tumble out of bed . . .

HACKER. It's Pain, is it?

PAIN *(walking round them)*. The speculators, on a little midnight trip . . .

STRUGGLE. 'e talks like Toplis, but 'e's got more wit than that.

PAIN. What's this? The union flag? Was ever an emblem so abused? If flags could speak they'd scream at the occasions they are lent to decorate.

HACKER. Come off it, Pain, 'o's side are you on?

PAIN.   I have a view. I have a view which says to murder Mr Hacker would not eradicate the Hackers, that to run about stamping on the despicable is not a fit occupation for a man who cares about his dignity.

HACKER.   I go along with that.

PAIN.   No. Nothing I say could you possibly go along with.

HACKER.   Modest, ain't he 'e? Can I get down, please?

PAIN.   Yes, and bring the banner.

BLEEDER *(climbing down with the skirt).*   I know what you're saying. You're saying people like me crop up like a smelly weed—*(He hops to the ground)* And you're a genius, all right?

PAIN.   Give me the skirt. *(He tosses it to* PAIN*)* I am a collector of defunct flags. Filled my study with the rags of empires I knocked down. Now I knock down Toplis' Republic of Reluctant Regiments. *(He opens it out)* Someone's coming. Run. *(They hurry away.* PAIN *pulls on the skirt)* Oh, God, I am never more myself than in another person's clothes . . . *(He starts to hurry out)*

MUSIC.   Oi! (PAIN *stops.* MUSIC, *on sentry-go, saunters a little nearer)* Angel. *(A step nearer)* Beauty Bum. *(Pause.* PAIN *has his back to* MUSIC*)* Comrade, may I—(PAIN *starts to run)* OI! *(He aims his rifle at the figure of* PAIN. *He freezes)* Don't be frightened. I am no fucking brute. Not a stuffer. Scrapped all that. My feelings are entirely spiritual— (PAIN *starts off again)* OI! *(and stops)* I wish you wouldn't wander, darling, comrade love. *(He goes nearer)* Please, may I appreciate you on a different plane? *(He looks at* PAIN*)* I don't think in my thirty-seven years I 'ave clapped eyes on better legs . . .

PAIN *(falsetto).*   I must go to a meeting.

MUSIC.   No, listen, comrade, I 'ave been digging 'oles for corpses all day long—

PAIN.   Sorry, got to—

MUSIC *(grabbing his shoulder).*   DON'T GO AWAY! Share a little warmth, will yer? Don't keep it back. I say 'ang Toplis and New Everythin' if— *(Pause)* the women are gonna keep it back . . .

PAIN.   Can I go, please?

MUSIC *(knowing).*   No, you endure me you strange bitch . . . *(with a cry* PAIN *tries to bolt, but* MUSIC *holds him)*

PAIN.   Oh, Christ!

MUSIC *lets out a roar of triumph and dropping his rifle, pulls* PAIN *off into the dark. The cries bring two figures hurrying onto the stage.*

SLIPPER/CASHIN *(pistols drawn).*   Where! Where! *(They dash about, crash into one another)* Where? Where?

At last PAIN *staggers in from the dark, collapses onto his knees. They look at him, he knows them. Pause.*

PAIN.   Oh, God, you're late . . .

CASHIN.   Been in Dublin.

SLIPPER.   Sorry.

CASHIN.   Had our hands a bit full there . . .

MUSIC *(emerging from the shadows).* Let's do it again! *(He sees* CASHIN *and* SLIPPER) 'o are these gentlemen? Waving their Webleys? You will terrify my conqueror, put 'im off 'is stroke!

CASHIN *(staring at* PAIN). Roger . . . he is in a skirt . . .

SLIPPER. Yes . . .

CASHIN. Why?

SLIPPER. Tell you later . . .

MUSIC *(touching* PAIN). Kind flesh 'e 'as, like convent girls I've nudged on English winters . . .

PAIN. I've not been touched. Nothing coarsens skin like skin, perishes it like passion . . .

MUSIC. No. You've oiled it.

PAIN. For my private joy.

MUSIC. Never! No privacy in flesh. We own nothing, but we shall possess each other, charm or poach it. Music's Law.

PAIN. The Great Democracy of Fuck . . .

MUSIC. Yes! Give us something for our sodding misery! (PAIN *gets to his feet, unsteadily. He starts to walk out, totters and falls in a faint.* SLIPPER *goes to help*) No! (SLIPPER *stops.* MUSIC *picks* PAIN *up*) Oh, angry little genius. I will carry you 'ome to your cot . . . *(He carries him off. Pause)*

SLIPPER. The Greatest Living Englishman—

CASHIN. Roger—

SLIPPER. The Spirit of the English race—

CASHIN. Not for us to reason why—

SLIPPER. Is BENT.

CASHIN. Roger—

SLIPPER. BENT. *(He looks at* CASHIN) I said how calm I am. I am calm. Only to think in my home I have a boy barely eleven for whom that man is—

CASHIN. All things good—

SLIPPER. And all things English—

CASHIN. Yes. *(Pause. He smiles)* That's all.

They go out.

ACT THREE

Scene One

A table and chairs. TRELLIS *is sitting on the table.* ERICA *is standing.*

ERICA.   You see, I actually don't like you very much.

TRELLIS.   That's all right.

ERICA.   No. It's not all right. Not really all right at all. I didn't like you very much when you were silent. Now you have a voice I dislike you more, if anything.

TRELLIS.   I understand that.

ERICA.   Particularly because you understand everything. It's one of the things about the New England which gets up my nose. This unnatural capacity for understanding one another. It jars my system because—let me finish—let me finish, please—I get a positive—thrill—from contradiction. I love antagonism. Pain, if you like. I would shrivel up without it. (*She looks at* TRELLIS, *direct*) Now that is utterly silly and I know what you're going to say—

TRELLIS.   A residual class characteristics—

ERICA.   How funny! I knew you would say that! The upper class struggling with its own sense of futility.

TRELLIS.   Yes. (*Pause*)

ERICA.   You are so predictable. Lovely. And predictable.

TRELLIS.   That don't make it untrue.

ERICA.   No! And that's even worse! When clichés are true, it must be time to quit!

TRELLIS.   Listen. Truth is very simple. Get it in your 'and, all right? Pick it up an' pass it round. Like Spangles, 'elp yerself, all right?

ERICA.   I love your slogans, but—

TRELLIS.   Do you? (*Pause*)

ERICA.   I'm very far gone, aren't I? Terribly far gone in my—whatever it is—my rot? I am a bit of a selfish hint. Resolve my contradictions, will you?

TRELLIS.   You don't want 'em solved.

ERICA.   Oh, don't I? I do. I do want happiness.

TRELLIS.   What's 'appiness got to do with it? New England ain't 'appiness.

ERICA.   It's not . . . ?

TRELLIS.   I'm not 'appy.

ERICA.   Then what are you doing it for?

TRELLIS.   Because there is a better thing than 'appiness. Because I'm sick of 'appiness, an' lookin' for it everywhere. I'm in a state where I don't even think about it.

ERICA.   That must be happiness!

TRELLIS.   I'm not interested in those questions because they're questions about self. I'm sick of self. My self and your self. When I came 'ere I was weeping for a sailor. A man I thought was the same as 'appiness. An' before 'im was a plumber. I thought 'e was 'appiness, too. But they never are, are they? Not 'appiness.

ERICA.   No. Something else, though? Feeling, perhaps?

TRELLIS.   Misery. An' little spurts of pleasure. Fuck that for 'appiness.

ERICA.   Yes! Good. Good! Fuck it! *(Pause)*

TRELLIS.   You are ruinin' Toplis. With your sticky love.

ERICA.   Am I?

TRELLIS.   You're makin' something small an' simple into an obsession.

ERICA.   Yes, I do do that. I turn everything into an obsession. Tea-drinking. Boxing. Underwear.

TRELLIS.   'e's missed three meetings of the Committee of Defence.

ERICA.   My God.

TRELLIS *(closing her eyes in anger)*.   Don't jeer. Don't jeer at us!

ERICA.   No—

TRELLIS.   I 'ave taken my life in my fingers, do you see that? 'ave picked it up an' started makin' it, is that funny?

ERICA.   No.

TRELLIS.   I 'ad feelings, lots of feelings, an' feelings got me started, but now I 'ave to find intelligence, and I dunno 'ow to, is that funny?

ERICA.   Not at all.

TRELLIS.   I get so much wrong I'm more often on my arse than on my feet, is that funny?

ERICA.   No.

TRELLIS.   Get ten things wrong for every one thing right, look stupid, contradict myself, if I didn't 'ave to think where to put my next foot I would weep, is that funny? (ERICA *shakes her head. Pause*) Toplis an' you. Munch, munch off one another's despair. Fuck an' giggle. Mould growin' up yer backs.

She goes out. TOPLIS *appears, places his arm round* ERICA'S *waist.* ERICA *is stiff and unyielding.*

ERICA.   Why don't you talk to me?

TOPLIS.   I do.

ERICA.   No, talk. *(Pause)* Not murmur. Talk. *(He looks at her)* I have stood here and been pelted with slogans, drenched in the spittle of her anguish and soaked in self-righteousness. She slops phrases like an overfilled bucket, and all of them originate in you. Why don't you talk?

TOPLIS.   What would a slogan do for you?

ERICA.   I don't know.

TOPLIS.   Slogans would spoil you.

ERICA.   How?

TOPLIS.   I don't itch for her. I itch for you. Though she walks upright now, and looks you in the eye, I don't itch.

ERICA.   Keep me urgent? Keep me ripe? *(Pause. She turns away)* I will not be made to feel my life is a little pool of piss!

TOPLIS *(shrugs)*.   You've said as much yourself.

ERICA.   That's different. My personal abuse. My self-laceration. Tear myself to ribbons if I like.

TOPLIS. Come here. I'll lick the age out of your face . . .

ERICA. I love, don't I? I love at least.

TOPLIS. Yes.

ERICA. I'll die for it. Or of it. Nothing else.

TOPLIS. I spent five years with women who believed that in the night, but in the morning got up while I slept to count their jewels. I grew used to it, the sound of shifting trinkets, the sight of their studiously curving naked backs poised over dressing-tables, wondering what I might have nicked . . .

ERICA. I have no jewels.

They embrace. HACKER enters, with a briefcase. He watches this.

HACKER. The co-ordinating committee, I suppose? This is the only co-ordination that goes on round 'ere. Co-ordination of the co-ordinators. Oh, open your co-ordinators and let my co-ordinator in! Everywhere yer look there are these two-man committees 'ard at work. Since they abolished prostitution, I 'ave been tripping over 'em. *(He coughs loudly)* The Co-ordinating Committee? 'alf past ten? (ERICA *and* TOPLIS *separate.* ERICA *walks off.* HACKER *sits.* TRELLIS *comes in with* DOWNCHILD, DITCH, ISTED *and* STRUGGLE, some carrying chairs) Good-morning! *(They look at him without greeting)*

TRELLIS. Sod good-morning, we are late again!

DOWNCHILD *(putting a clock on the table).* Not quite late, Sandra . . .

TRELLIS. Soon will be if we carry on like this. We ain't getting enough done at these meetings, are we? I wanna bring that up.

ISTED. Where's my chair?

TRELLIS *(to* STRUGGLE). Make a note, Rowena, will yer? Time spent in committee?

ISTED *(to* DOWNCHILD). I think yer in my chair, mate.

TRELLIS. Stan, we're waitin' to begin!

ISTED. I know, but—

TRELLIS. 'ave another seat! *(He sits)* I wanna discuss the lack of proper time-keeping. I wanna propose penalties for absences.

DITCH. Any Other Business, ain't it?

TRELLIS. No. Not Any Other Business. No one listens to Any Other Business. I propose abolishin' it.

TOPLIS. That comes under Any Other Business, doesn't it? The abolition of Any Other Business?

TRELLIS. Where's Jane? Where's Eddie? 'o's seen Jane? *(Pause)*

HACKER. Co-ordinating. In the sand dunes. *(She glares at him)* Beg pardon.

TRELLIS. Can't wait any longer. Session's open, then. (MUSIC *enters*) You're late.

MUSIC. Sorry.

TRELLIS. Sorry. That poor fuckin' word.

MUSIC *(sitting).* Beg pardon, then.

TRELLIS. Listen, I am becomin' like a rough ol' shouter, but we must keep time.

MUSIC. Yes.

TRELLIS.   One day, we'll come in casual, drift in as it suits us. And one day
I will find a little sweet old voice—
STRUGGLE *(opening papers).*   The fifteenth meeting of the Supplies and
Provisioning Committee—
ISTED *(interrupting).*   I don't think this gentleman is permitted at this
meeting. I mean, not 'ave a seat.
HACKER.   Oh, aren't I? Very sorry.
TRELLIS.   Thankyou, Stan.—Would you be kind enough to sit over there?
HACKER.   Certainly.
MUSIC *(looking at him).*   Funny, ain't it? Three weeks ago I would 'ave put
a bullet into 'im . . .
TOPLIS.   And now you lick his tonsils. New England is so rich in irony . . .
TRELLIS.   If you got a point, you will 'ave a chance to raise it.
HACKER.   I would like to say, come the end of the morning, one day I was
rubbish, but the next, they found a use for me.
DITCH.   Shuddup, please!
TRELLIS.   The proposal of the Committee for supplies is that Mr Hacker
be invited to act as Commissioner for Food, on the grounds we lack
sufficient expertise. There was a paper on it. 'o's against?
TOPLIS.   Me.
TRELLIS.   Would you like to speak, then? And will you watch the clock,
please? There's a foreign affairs meeting at twelve. *(Pause. TOPLIS stands)*
TOPLIS.   Because we are inept, it's been proposed, as a temporary
measure, to invite Mr Alfred Hacker, late of Hacker's General Stores, to
act as overseer in the matter of supply. Strictly within a controlled profit
margin. Strictly under the eye of this committee. A high degree of strictness
to contain this strictly avaricious man—
HACKER.   Objection!
TRELLIS.   You ain't allowed to object.
HACKER.   I still do . . .
TOPLIS.   And why? Because we cannot function without his expertise!
Because his skill in nosing out what he has previously concealed makes him
indispensible! Because his shuddering itch for gain—
DITCH.   'ooray!
TOPLIS.   makes him, like some diseased bloodhound, scratch at the sand
more wildly than we can in our common need! Because the self-soiling of
grasp and greed must triumph over the ability to share, we must have
Alfred Hacker back, though he dirties the air with his cacky breath—
HACKER.   DO I 'AVE TER SIT 'ERE AND—
TOPLIS.   We must have him over us! I am opposed to it!
DITCH.   'OORAY!
HACKER.   Disgraceful. (DITCH *and* DOWNCHILD *clap enthusiastically*
TOPLIS *sits*) Dis–fucking–graceful.
TRELLIS.   That's not an argument—
DITCH.   'OORAY!
TRELLIS.   Whatcha cheerin' for? That's not an argument!
TOPLIS.   I didn't win them by arguments. I put magic on their lips.
MUSIC.   Magic some fuckin' dinner, then!

STRUGGLE. Out of order, darling—

MUSIC. We got no grub, that is the argument.

STRUGGLE. Through the chair, please—

MUSIC. Through what?

STRUGGLE. Me. I'm the chair.

MUSIC. I don't wanna go through you—

TRELLIS. Eddie!

MUSIC. I don't wanna go through 'er—

TRELLIS. We are struggling 'ere, ain't we? We gotta know, what we can do, and what we can't. 's no good wipin' our noses on silk 'andkerchiefs if we can't eat.

DOWNCHILD. Vote! Move we vote!

MUSIC. I ain't spoken.

TRELLIS. What are we when it comes down to it? What are we? A few 'undred soldiers and three barrack pros.

TOPLIS. If you persist in thinking you are nothing, you will be nothing—

MUSIC. I speak! I speak! *(Pause)*

DITCH. Vote!

MUSIC. Shuddup! I wanna speak! *(Pause)* I ask yer, 'o's more dangerous? The devil yer know, or the devil yer don't? 'cos there is a devil 'ere yer know, 'an one yer don't. One 'o tells you you are gods an' cannot lay a bleedin' toffee on the desk, an' one 'o 'as a knack for fillin' plates. I tell yer, if we 'ave no dinner we are done. See, I don't talk no magic. I say lick Hacker's crevices if we 'ave to. There's more nourishment in 'is arse crack than there is in Mr Toplis' words.

TOPLIS. Oh, Hacker, I hear the laughter rolling round the inside of your face—

ISTED. First we use 'im, then we kick 'im off.

TRELLIS. I move we vote!

MUSIC. Seconded.

STRUGGLE. Those in favour of giving Mr Hacker authority in matters of supply, please raise your hands. (TRELLIS, MUSIC, ISTED, DOWNCHILD *raise their hands*) Those against? (DITCH *and* TOPLIS) Carried.

TOPLIS. I resign from this committee.

MUSIC. What for.

TOPLIS *(standing)*. I resign.

MUSIC. What fuckin' for!

TRELLIS. The meeting is suspended.

HACKER *(rising)*. Where does that leave me, then, please? (TRELLIS *leans on the table in despair*)

DITCH. Got it, ain't yer?

HACKER. And will I be notified officially? Of my status in the New England? I ask because—(DITCH *goes out*. HACKER *looks to another*) because the actual figure—my percentage—has yet to be negotiated, I believe?

STRUGGLE *indicates he should go. He goes out.* DOWNCHILD, ISTED,
STRUGGLE *leave, carrying chairs. Pause.*

TRELLIS.   We 'ave so little time . . . we can't afford all that . . . resigning
stuff. . . that pride an' honour business . . . my precious this . . . my principle
of that . . . got to get down in the dirt now . . . *(He turns to go)* Oh, don't go
off! All stiff an' rigid! *(He stops)*

TOPLIS.   Stiff? No. I go to where my magic counts. *(She looks at him,
gathers her things, leaves.* TALLBOY *wheels himself in)*

TALLBOY.   Give us a trick.

TOPLIS *(turning to him).*   Your daughter has had all my tricks.

TALLBOY.   Go on. Give us a trick.

TOPLIS *(going near to him, taking out a pistol).* Take wand! *(He holds*
TALLBOY'S *head)* Take dirty old Omdurman lancers, brothel sniffing
leather back—

TALLBOY.   HEY!

TOPLIS.   white-with-sinning English head and—

TALLBOY.   HEY! (TOPLIS *comes close to his ear)*

TOPLIS.   Oh, do I frighten you?

TALLBOY.   HEY!

TOPLIS.   Oh, do I, ribbon tit? Staring through your cataracts, sun winking
in the great dry cellars of your brain? If I shot you, would it crumble, go all
powder like a blown egg ninety years on some museum shelf? No blood?
No muck? WHAT! *(He bends over him grotesquely)* But no . . . he lives . . .
he lives . . . *(He strokes his head in a parody of affection)* They can be
bleeding everywhere, but this one lives . . . *(Pause.* TOPLIS *kisses it)*

TALLBOY.   What people will do to you, when you are helpless in a chair.
When they think you neither hear nor speak. Pinch you. Poke you.
Whisper filth. The things fermenting in their souls. Crisp wives urgent with
misdemeanours. Mad diplomats. Nurses who bite . . .

TOPLIS *(moves away. He shudders convulsively, his eyes closed).* If it
relieves you, speak . . . (TOPLIS *gathers himself, turns to go)* Isn't it time
you had a stroke?

Scene Two

Night-time in the Governor's garden. A table covered in a white cloth and laid.
SLIPPER *and* CASHIN *in evening dress stand behind the chairs, alone.*
SLIPPER *is feeling his pulse.*

SLIPPER.   In France, on night patrol, I shuddered, didn't you? Heart in
mouth and poop at very tip of bowel? But now, pulse very slightly up, and
that not fear, but thrill . . . how about you?

CASHIN.   Nothing.

SLIPPER.   Really rather want to kill.

CASHIN.   Yes.

SLIPPER.   Put in dum-dum, Don. Split nose 45.

CASHIN.   Yes.

SLIPPER. Germans used to crucify anyone found using that. Honourable people, huns.

CASHIN. I think I want to give this up.

SLIPPER. What?

CASHIN. You heard.

SLIPPER. Not now.

CASHIN. Not now, no. When we get back. Think I've slain widely for the crown now. Want a lovely green desk in a bank.

SLIPPER. Nerves talking.

CASHIN. Listen—

SLIPPER. Loquacious nerves.

CASHIN. Want a desk, with bums of typists going by, click-click heels and shaded lamps. So when the kids say what did you do today, I'll say in truth, I did—whatever it is that they do in banks.

SLIPPER. I'm saying pass the salt. All right?

CASHIN. I mean it, Michael.

SLIPPER. Pass the salt.

CASHIN. All right! (ERICA *enters, radiant and pushing* TALLBOY)

ERICA. What a gorgeous evening! Have you looked at the clouds? The clouds? The red clouds? The tinted, rather pinkish clouds? We don't get clouds like that except when rain is imminent, but you wouldn't know that, would you? Strangers couldn't know that, couldn't share our little pleasures, I could almost get my watercolours out, but I doubt if I could catch it, or if I did, who would believe it? They'd say you rather overdid the red, those clouds there, much too red! Anyway, you don't want me painting at the dinner table, do you? I paint rather like a monkey, have you seen monkeys painting? They say they would paint just as well as Titian if you waited long enough. Oh, do sit down! I say Titian, God knows why, I could have said—well, insert your favourite painter. Mine isn't Titian, actually, it's Renoir. No, it isn't. Now, why did I say Renoir? I don't have a favourite painter. No, you sit there, SIT THERE! No, opposite! I like you to be opposite! I have no favourite painter, who is yours?

SLIPPER. Churchill.

ERICA. I don't know him, is he very good? My dad, my poor old dad, will sit there, will sit well away from you because he—well, he gets it—you know old men and their grub—(TOPLIS *comes in, goes to sit*) No, I am sitting there!

SLIPPER (*standing*). Shall we—

ERICA. You sit exactly where you are and I will—(TOPLIS *persists*) I'm SITTING THERE! (TOPLIS *moves round, so he is beside* CASHIN) Entertaining! Do so little entertaining now! Not that we did much in the old days, did we, dad? Call it the old days, not so very old, are they? Mr Cashin, Mr Slipper—Mr Toplis. Mr Cashin? Mr Slipper? Is that right?

SLIPPER. Correct.

ERICA. Cashin and Slipper! They are—what are they? Such a long word—what—

SLIPPER. Demographers.

ERICA.   Demographers! Lovely!
TOPLIS.   Demographers?

YOUNG *enters, in a waiter's jacket, with a tureen of soup.*

YOUNG.   Soup, Comrades?
ERICA.   Thank you, put it there.
YOUNG.   There?
ERICA.   Anywhere. *(He goes out)* Do you like soup? Cold soup? We are
   down to cold soups in all their multitide of forms and flavours, cold grass
   soup, cold leaf soup, cold seed soup, of course I do exaggerate, wantonly
   exaggerate, but things are not that lavish, to be frank—
TOPLIS.   There are no people here.
ERICA.   I keep that seat for Mr Hacker, Mr Hacker will be joining us, and
   should you want to mutter any protest on the subject of provisions, mutter
   them to him, he is food commissioner, and very—
TOPLIS.   There are no people here.
ERICA.   Why do you keep saying that? You have said that, hasn't he? Said
   that at least once?
SLIPPER.   No . . .
ERICA.   What? No what? No soup? Shall I just serve and sod Mr Hacker?
   (She begins dishing up)
SLIPPER.   No, there are no people.
ERICA *(offering a bowl).*   Dad? I still say Dad, as if he would reply or
   something, but he won't now, will he?
TOPLIS.   Grotesque. We get a hydrologist in a waterless country and now
   demographers where there are no people.
SLIPPER.   The British at the peak of their futility.
TOPLIS.   So they would like us all to think.
ERICA.   Ah, Hacker! I think I hear him crashing through the undergrowth,
   well, not undergrowth exactly, if ever there was a place could do with a
   little undergrowth—
TOPLIS.   The hydrologist is dead.
ERICA.   Good evening!
HACKER.   Good evening, Miss. Good evening, gentlemen.
ERICA.   There is your seat! *(He sits)* Oh, this is nice! This is nice, isn't it?
HACKER.   Cold soup!
ERICA.   Cold soup. If you would dig up some of your secret supplies of
   dried eggs, yeast and curry—
HACKER.   The old myth. God bless it.
ERICA.   These gentlemen have walked here through the desert!
TOPLIS.   Ostensibly in search of blacks.
ERICA.   Christ, I'm hot! Who minds if I undo these buttons? This is a pre-
   republic dress! Don't worry, shan't show much, no one to get excited! Just
   flash the scrawny neck a bit . . .
HACKER.   All the black faces here are underground.
ERICA.   Must you talk about typhoid, Mr Hacker? You are typhoid mad—
   (HACKER *reaches over, between* ERICA *and* SLIPPER *and* CASHIN) I
   WISH YOU WOULDN'T LEAN ACROSS THE TABLE!

HACKER.   Did I? Beg pardon. Wanted the salt.

ERICA.   Ask. Ask for it.

HACKER.   Salt, please.

SLIPPER.   We did demography in Ireland. Before coming here.

TOPLIS.   The figures fell, I take it, between your coming and your going?

SLIPPER.   Oddly. Oddly, yes.

ERICA.   What do you believe in, Mr Cashin? Love or politics?

CASHIN.   My wife.

ERICA.   And which is that?

HACKER *(leaning)*.   Is that pepper?

ERICA.   WILL YOU NOT KEEP JUMPING UP! *(She smiles)* I can't see Mr Cashin.

SLIPPER.   We really are—rather—cramped—up here—

CASHIN.   Elbows—

SLIPPER.   Clashing . . .

ERICA.   I love to face my guests, I love their faces, we do not see real faces, not faces which are so very pink and fresh, we are—aren't we—such very lizardy old things—and you—so damp and pink . . .

SLIPPER.   Ireland.

ERICA.   Must be. I have no complexion any more, though I've rubbed God knows what creams and jellies into it . . . goat sperm included when we had a goat . . . the regimental goat this was . . . I was forever at its . . . whatever happened to that goat . . . was it . . . *(She dries. Everyone but HACKER has finished eating. Pause)*

TOPLIS.   I think what I hate most about—demographers—*(He looks at CASHIN and SLIPPER)* the class in England known as—the demographic class—is its misery. I spent five years on the Riviera, a louse clinging in the groin of English demography, and I never knew a class of women so inclined to weep. *(Pause)*

CASHIN.   My wife was two weeks on the Riviera.

SLIPPER.   Don—

CASHIN.   The Hotel Beauregard. Know it?

SLIPPER.   Don—

TOPLIS.   Know it? I've laboured in all its hundred rooms.

CASHIN.   Mrs Rosemary Cashin, of Twickenham.

SLIPPER.   Don—

CASHIN.   Tiny hands and tiny feet? *(Pause. CASHIN stares at TOPLIS. SLIPPER suddenly stands up)*

SLIPPER.   Pass the salt, please! (CASHIN *does not react.* HACKER *looks for the salt)*

TOPLIS.   Frantic, devouring, little hip?

SLIPPER.   Pass the salt, please!

HACKER.   Yer've already got it, yer silly—

SLIPPER.   I know I have. PASS THE SALT!

CASHIN.   Hip? *(He is staring fixedly at TOPLIS)* Hip?

SLIPPER *(starting to draw his pistol)*.   THE SALT! THE SALT!

ERICA *is quicker than* SLIPPER, *and draws her pistols from under the table.*
HACKER *lets out a cry of terror and dives under the table.*

ERICA.   I'LL SHOOT! I'LL SHOOT! I WILL! I'LL SHOOT! *(She covers both men. There is a silence)*
CASHIN.   Oh, God . . . sorry, Roger . . .
ERICA.   I am going to shoot you. I am. I really am.
CASHIN.   I have a child, a boy of eleven. A very lovely boy, with such fine eyelashes.
SLIPPER.   Don—
CASHIN.   Who runs to me along our hall, and hugs my knees, and has such firm little limbs—
SLIPPER.   SHUT UP, DON.
CASHIN.   Please. He loves me.
SLIPPER.   Stand up, man. Stand up.

He sobs. ERICA *fires the pistols.* CASHIN *and* SLIPPER *tumble backwards.*
ERICA *lets out a terrible cry, shuddering uncontrollably.*

ERICA.   Oh, look at me! Oh, look at me!
TALLBOY.   What's that? What's that?
HACKER *(staggering from under the table).*   Help! Help!

He is covered in their blood. Madly, he tears off the tablecloth and starts wiping himself with it. TOPLIS *does not move.*

ERICA.   Have I done it? Have I?
HACKER.   HE–LP!
ERICA.   HAVE I DONE IT?
TOPLIS.   Yes . . .
ERICA.   Hold me, then! Oh, hold me, then!
HACKER *(running off).*   MUR–DER! MUR–DER!
ERICA.   Why don't you hold me? *(Pause)* Why don't you?
TOPLIS.   Erica, don't you see how little I have to give? *(Pause)*
ERICA.   Give that, then!
TOPLIS.   Only my mean, shrivelled, under-the-bedclothes thing . . .
ERICA.   Why are you saying this?
TOPLIS.   I have to conjure with them, Erica. Like the women on the boulevard. See what I can drive them to. In their madness, I taste something like life . . .

MUSIC *hurries in, bearing an armful of rifles.*

MUSIC.   The Australians are landin' on the beach! The same sheep-shaggers who would boil Turks' 'eads, and sent us bleatin' back to Flanders! Their boots'll scuff ol' Ditch's grass a bit! 'ere, cop a rifle! *(TOPLIS doesn't move)* Christ, Toplis, you look as full of joy as a thrice-used johnny . . . *(TOPLIS indicates the dead men.* MUSIC *walks round the table, looks)* Well, you made a proper trifle of their 'eads. *(He offers a rifle from his stack)*

TOPLIS.   Eddie, don't get stuck on some bawdy bayonet . . . (MUSIC *stops still, stares*) I know a man has got a nightclub in Caracas . . . (ERICA *lets out a sob and a wail*)

MUSIC.   Come again . . . *(Pause)* You thing . . . Come again . . .

TOPLIS.   I tap, see . . . *(He gets up, starts to dance)* While keeping three balls in the air . . . *(He takes them out of his pocket, begins juggling)*

MUSIC.   WHERE IS YOUR FUCKIN' HONOUR, YOU! *(He stops)*

TOPLIS.   Isn't that the thing you find in abattoirs? Gurgling down the sluice?

Pause, then MUSIC chucks all the rifles onto the floor, with a clatter, but for one, which he holds. Pause.

MUSIC.   Your knees. (TOPLIS *kneels readily*)

TOPLIS.   With four balls I can sustain illusions of—(*He catches them again. His head hangs, as if for execution.* MUSIC *rattles the bolt of his rifle*)

MUSIC.   Talk, then. I am no military policeman, an' my ears are dry . . .

ERICA.   Give him to me. He is no earthly use to you. Or anyone . . .

MUSIC.   No, talk! (*Pause.* TOPLIS *shakes his head*) Oh, Christ, I do believe he is ashamed . . . (PAIN *enters. He is holding the body of* TRELLIS. *They see him*)

PAIN.   She would lecture them, told the blaspheming Anzacs keep their voices down, in the New England people had no need to shout . . . (MUSIC *lets out a terrible cry of despair.* ERICA *goes to take it*) DON'T TOUCH 'ER! (*He goes to the body, takes it from* PAIN) We ain't mocked . . . We ain't mocked, see . . . ?

He draws her face to his, kisses it. Lights snap out.

Fair Slaughter

Fair Slaughter was first performed at the Royal Court Theatre, 13 June 1977 with the following cast:

OLD GOCHER	Max Wall
LEARY	John Thaw
YOUNG GOCHER	Nick Edmett
STAVELEY	Tony Matthews
TOVARISH	David Jackson
MOIRA	Judith Liebert
DOCTOR	Robert Gary
MELANIE	Jan Chappell
PORTER	Tony Halfpenny
FIREMAN	Robin Meredith

Directed by Stuart Burge

Scene One

The hospital, Wandsworth. A single iron bed containing GOCHER, *asleep under a grey blanket.* LEARY, *a prison officer, comes in.*

LEARY. He did WHAT. He did WHAT! With a PISSPOT? Brained an old bloke with a PISSPOT? What are old men coming to? Where is your DIGNITY? (*He stands near the bed, bending to* GOCHER's *ear*).

GOCHER. Leave off.

LEARY. A twisted grandad. The horror of the old folk's home. England's oldest living murderer. Let's have a look at yer.

GOCHER. Give us a bit of peace, son.

LEARY. DON'T SON ME! DON'T PATRONIZE ME, YOU OLD KILLER! (*Pause. He stands back.)* Right. Let's have a look at yer. COME ON!

GOCHER. This is the hospital.

LEARY. And that's all right, is it? Because this is the hospital. You can do what you like in the hospital. Like kipping all day and crapping in chamber pots, because this is the hospital. You have just been in one hospital and look what you did there. You degrade the whole idea of hospital! (*Pause. He walks up and down.)* Anyway, this is Wandsworth. It's not like any old hospital. It is the prison hospital. And they are scarcely hospitals at all, I tell you that. They are firstly prisons and only second hospitals, whereas hospitals are firstly hospitals, and only second prisons. All right? Do you follow me? GRANDAD!

GOCHER. I follow yer.

LEARY. All right, then. Let's have a look at yer.

Pause.

GOCHER. You are degrading me.

LEARY. Correct. I am degrading you.

GOCHER. I won't be degraded. I protest.

LEARY *looks at him for a few moments.*

LEARY. All this about degrading. I hear so much about degrading. My ears are singing with the protests of criminals who will not be degraded. It is all the fucking rage, how criminals should not be degraded. When they have stuck their things up little girls. When they have put bombs in the public bar. It is the way of the world. It is human life, is degradation. My dog will tell you about his degradation. The universe is degradation. When these bleeders who have done vile things tell me they will not be degraded, I become a fan of it! (*Pause.)* So I want to look at you. And you stuff your protest up your arse.

GOCHER. I'll catch my death.

LEARY. You're all right. You're in the hospital.

GOCHER. Have pity on a poor old sod!

LEARY. Turn the sheets back.

GOCHER. I demand to see the governor!

LEARY. DO IT!

GOCHER *(clasping the blanket to his chin).* No.

Pause. LEARY goes towards the bed.

LEARY. I will see you, ol' fellar. I have made up my mind. (*He goes to the bed, grabs the blanket and rips it right back. GOCHER lets out a squeal. He is lying perfectly still, but in a humped position, as if lying on something. Pause.*) You are concealing something. Aren't you? Like every other individual in this place, squealing about degradation is a means to something else. This principles rubbish is a pretext for another act of treachery. What are you hiding! (GOCHER *doesn't move.* LEARY *shakes his head.*) Christ, in a prison every little prejudice you have, it gets confirmed. And confirmed. (*He holds out his hand.* GOCHER *shakes his head.*)

GOCHER. Don't come near me, son. I will murder you.

LEARY. What is it? Whisky?

GOCHER *(contemptuously).* Whisky . . .

LEARY. An explosive, is it?

GOCHER. You might say that.

Pause.

LEARY. I shall have to have it, shan't I? I shall have to have a little look.

GOCHER. I have had this with me for fifty years. No police bastard is going to take it off me now. That is an oath.

LEARY. I am throbbing with curiosity.

GOCHER. You throb.

Long pause. They glare at one another.

LEARY. I think you are going to get uncomfortable. I think your biscuity old spine is gonna ache.

GOCHER. Let it.

Long pause, then with a shrug, LEARY *turns to go out. Just as he leaves, he spins round again.*

LEARY. Ah–ha!

GOCHER. I'm cold! I'm bloody cold!

LEARY. You would be. In this draught.

GOCHER. Haven't you heard of hypothermia? (LEARY *just looks at him.*) Oh, Christ, my back! (*With a groan,* GOCHER *sinks back, pulling out from under him a glass-stoppered bottle.*) Oh, Gawd, tortured to death in an English gaol!

LEARY. You lay it on a bit thick, Gocher. *(He comes back to the bed.)* May I look?

GOCHER.   I have to get out of here! Help me to get out of here!

LEARY.   I thought you got eight years. *(He takes the jar, looks at it.)* Oh, fucking hell . . .

GOCHER.   Help me. Help me.

LEARY.   Oh, bloody hell . . . *(He holds the jar up to the light. It contains a human hand.)* What the human mind will sink to. Whose is it?

GOCHER.   MY YOUTH, MY BLOODY YOUTH!

Scene Two

Instantly the sound of a thin, icy wind. A SOLDIER comes in, holding a rifle. He is clad in a white snow camouflage outfit over a uniform, 1920's style. He is so stuffed with rags, he moves only with difficulty. Over the wind, sound of approaching cavalry.

YOUNG GOCHER.   The Cossacks! I can hear the Cossacks! It's the Cossacks! Blimey, sir! *(The sound gets louder. YOUNG GOCHER vaguely aims his rifle and pulls the trigger. It only clicks.)* Oh, fuck! *(He drops the rifle and screws himself into a ball. Horses thunder by. Odd shots are heard. After a few moments, he lifts his head.)* Russia. 1920. Somewhere in the Arctic wastes. This is a crusade, Mr. Churchill says. Against bandits who hate families and property, the twin tits of the Goddess Civilization whose image we carry on campaign. Think of the Tsar, our C.O. says, as you wield the bayonet. Think of his daughters as you thrust, those long-haired beauties who might have made a good fuck for an English prince, now mutilated in a cellar, murdered by the BOL—SHE—VIKS! *(Pause.)* The English army. To within an ace of Petersburg. Saw the chimneys smoking. Officers predicting whether Lenin would be hung or shot. But then a cold spell, and our rifle bolts were frozen hard. The tanks seized up. When we were sweeping all before us. Home for Christmas, they had said. And the Reds do not take prisoners! This FUCKING CAPITALIST OIL!

The sound of thundering hooves again, and yelling. Staggering to his feet, GOCHER makes an undignified retreat.

Scene Three

The Prison Hospital. LEARY is examining the jar.

LEARY.   You have done another murder. A youthful crime of which this is the souvenir. Quite likely you have been a lifelong murderer, keeping grizzly relics. Is that true? (GOCHER *just looks at him.* LEARY *walks round with the jar.*) Somewhere there is an arm to which this is attached. Or more specifically, an arm bone. Or perhaps the bone itself has turned to dust. You would have seen to that, I expect, with acid. Was it acid? You're not obliged to say, of course.

GOCHER. I'm not obliged.

LEARY. All murder remains punishable. Up to the decease of the perpetrator. There is no escape from the law except by death.

GOCHER. I'm seventy-five, I'm not afraid of death. In the old men's ward they were all scared to death.

LEARY. Don't blame 'em, with you in there.

GOCHER. They were afraid of it because they'd lived such timid little lives. Something in 'em was crying out at the injustice of it, how they hadn't lived and therefore shouldn't be allowed to die. Forty years had gone and none of 'em had noticed it. They could remember nothing but the birthdays of their children and their holidays. *(Pause.)* Well, I am not like that. I am ready for it. But first I have to get that hand back.

LEARY. Get the hand back?

GOCHER. Where it belongs. It does not belong here. It is torture for it to be here.

LEARY. And where does it belong, then? If not here?

GOCHER. Russia.

LEARY. Russia? It is a Russian hand then, is it? It's a bit of communist?

Pause.

GOCHER. Listen to me, son.

LEARY. Not so much of the son, eh?

GOCHER. Will you listen to me?

LEARY. I might.

GOCHER. For Christ's sake I am talking to you as a human being! Will you bring yerself down from there! Open yer fucking ears and listen to a man who's flesh and blood and chuck all this what you might do and might not because of your sodding uniform. I'm asking you to be a man and listen to me. Do you see that? It is never easy to be just a man, but it is worth it, even for a minute. Try it. Open yer mind to me!

Pause. LEARY *looks at him.*

LEARY. All right. I am a fair geezer. You will find that out as time goes by.

Pause, then he goes to GOCHER *and covers him with the blanket. Blackout.*

Scene Four

A room in the British barracks, Murmansk, 1920. Lying on an iron bed, wrists hand-cuffed to the bed rail, YOUNG GOCHER *in vest, trousers and braces, puttees and boots.*

YOUNG GOCHER. The barracks. Murmansk. 1920.

An OFFICER *enters, in scarf, greatcoat, balaclava helmet under cap.*

STAVELEY. Cold. Bloody cold. Bitingly bloody cold. *(He stamps his feet.)* Funny how one's always on about the cold. When one know it's cold. When there's nothing new about it. When it's permanently minus seventeen. I wonder if Napoleon kept on about it. In 1812. Was it a topic in the Grand Army, I wonder? Are you cold?

YOUNG GOCHER. I have gone numb.

STAVELEY. Sir.

YOUNG GOCHER. Sir. I have gone numb.

STAVELEY. No tunic? No shirt?

YOUNG GOCHER. No, sir.

STAVELEY. Took 'em away, did they?

YOUNG GOCHER. Sir.

STAVELEY. I have a report. It says, I quote—*(he takes a paper from his pocket)* 7131 Gocher makes persistent use of the expression Capitalist. Is that true, Gocher? Do you use that word?

YOUNG GOCHER. I have done, sir.

STAVELEY. Why, I wonder?

YOUNG GOCHER. Descriptive, sir.

STAVELEY. But why?

YOUNG GOCHER. It is a word, sir.

STAVELEY. It is a word. Of course it is. It is a perfectly good word. Only I wonder why you use it. You being, as you are, a private soldier, and this word, this particular word, not being all that common usage. That's all. *(He smiles. Pause.)*

YOUNG GOCHER. It is an adjective.

STAVELEY. Fair point. It is an adjective. But to take me, as an example, a fairly ordinary example, I am an educated chap. I have had, for better or worse, an education at a school—a very good school—a better school than you I think we can say without a trace of snobbery, but utterly objectively—and as an educated man I say to you it is a word I don't think I have ever used. It is not for me a very familiar adjective. Can you explain that? *(Long pause.)* Can you explain why you appear to use it and I don't? Me being perfectly normal, having the gift of speech and so on. Can you say?

Long pause.

YOUNG GOCHER. It cropped up.

STAVELEY. It cropped up. Someone said it?

YOUNG GOCHER. I thought it was . . . I liked the sound of it . . .

STAVELEY. Go on.

YOUNG GOCHER. It sounded right.

Pause.

STAVELEY. Yes, it does have a sort of—I like the sound of it myself—but the crux of it, I think, Gocher, is not the sound but what we mean by it. Do you see that? The meaning we attach to it. *(Pause.)* Gocher.

Pause.

YOUNG GOCHER. We are the Capitalist Army, aren't we?

Pause. The OFFICER puts away the paper, goes towards the door. He turns.

STAVELEY. You will be sent home. You will be dishonourably discharged. Until such time as there is a boat available you will be kept here in irons on a bread and water diet. *(Pause.)* That is how the Capitalist Army treats its traitors. In the Communist Army they would have hammered bullet cases through your eyes. *(He turns and starts to go out.)*

YOUNG GOCHER. Don't go! Don't go! *(The* OFFICER *stops. Pause.)* Walking out. With yer nose up. In yer warm togs. Righteous.

STAVELEY. You are going home. You are taking your infection to your family, to your workplace, where it will rub off on your fellows. I would do society a service if I shot you. But there is a thing called Civilization. And that is why we are here. And that is why we relied on you, as we relied on all our soldiers, to be a happy band for Civilization. You have betrayed that trust. You have joined the wreckers and the death-dealers.

YOUNG GOCHER. That isn't it.

STAVELEY. It is it. It is it precisely.

YOUNG GOCHER. I will help you.

STAVELEY. How dare you.

YOUNG GOCHER. Let me. Let me.

STAVELEY. You cringing bastard.

YOUNG GOCHER. Don't let all that shit stick to—

STAVELEY. Shut up!

YOUNG GOCHER. All that vomit about—

STAVELEY. SHUT UP! SHUT UP! SHUT UP! *(He stamps his foot hysterically for a moment.* GOCHER *looks at him with amazement. Pause. The* OFFICER *recovers his equanimity.)* Your superiority. It is really—vile. It's vile. *(He goes out.)*

Pause.

YOUNG GOCHER. So I sat. I sat and I waited. And in my bread and water I read GOCHER, IN THE FURNACE OF EXPERIENCE YOU HAVE FORGED AN IDEAL. All from the knowledge of a cheapjack's lubricating oil that froze . . .

Pause. Suddenly, a man tumbles head over heels through the doors, as if flung violently. He rolls into a heap and lies there. He is wearing a peaked cap, tattered overalls and boots. Very tentatively, he unwinds, staring at GOCHER *all the time. He squats on his heels. Suddenly, he extends a hand.*

TOVARISH. Tovarish! (GOCHER *just looks at him. The man repeats the action.)* Tovarish!

GOCHER *sees the light.*

YOUNG GOCHER *(thrusting his hand as far as the iron will allow).* Com-rade!

The man gets up, hurries over and clasps GOCHER's *hand. They grin.*

TOVARISH. Za shto tibyaa syoda? Za shto tibyaa syoda? (GOCHER *shakes his head.)* Mileetsia zatsappala? (GOCHER *shakes his head.)* Ograbil stolyi kovau? Pryamuh na myaysti nakreeli?

YOUNG GOCHER.   No . . . sorry . . . no . . .

They sit silently for some time.

TOVARISH.   Ti popoll ny toda mozhet? Ninyeftyo vrayna, znadchet?
YOUNG GOCHER *(shrugging).*   Not a word. Not the foggiest. *(Pause.)*
Hopeless . . .

After a few moments the man tries again.

TOVARISH.   Chetyatt nass oonitch tozhit, na pralataryat ni oonitch
tozhish . . .
YOUNG GOCHER.   Come again!
TOVARISH.   Oonassyee barotsya chemyast—
YOUNG GOCHER.   No, no, what you just said. *(The man stops.)* What
you just said.
TOVARISH.   Chetyatt nass oonitch tozhit?
YOUNG GOCHER.   No, no . . . what you just said . . .

The man tries again.

TOVARISH.   Na pralataryat ni oonitch tozhish—
YOUNG GOCHER.   That's it! That's me! Me! Me! *(He points to himself.)*
Proletariat. That's me!
TOVARISH.   Pralataryat!
YOUNG GOCHER.   Da! da!
TOVARISH.   Sovietskai veegraaet!
YOUNG GOCHER.   Sovietska! Da! da! Proletariatska! sovietska! da! da!
TOVARISH *(grinning with inspiration).*   Ley—enin!
YOUNG GOCHER.   Oh, yes, oh, yes, Lenin!
TOVARISH.   Vladimir Ilyich Lyenin!
YOUNG GOCHER *(shaking his irons).*   First rate! First rate!!
TOVARISH.   Trotsky . . .
YOUNG GOCHER.   Trotsky! Trotsky, da, da! *(They both laugh out loud,
raising their fists in the party salute. Suddenly the man puts his fingers to
his lips to order silence. GOCHER watches as the man goes to the door,
peers to see if they are being watched, the returns and carries out the
following dumbshow. He occupies the whole floor. First, he pretends to be
an engine, puffing and moving his arms like pistons. GOCHER watches,
transfixed.)* Engine! *(The man goes on.)* Engine! *(The man stops, indicates
more to come. He again puffs like the engine, up and down.)* Engine . . .
*(Then he raises his arms like guns and makes a shooting sound. Then he
becomes an engine again, then repeats the shooting, on the move.)* Guns.
Guns. Engine. Guns *(The man puffs on.)* Engine again. *(The man whistles
like an engine.)* Train . . . guns . . . Armoured train! I get it! Armoured
train! *(The man stops, points to himself.)* You. On an armoured train. You.
Bang! Bang! You. Bang! Bang! *(The man shakes his hands to dismiss this.
Then he goes on to mime engine driving, looking as if out of the cab
window, and pulling the whistle handle. All the time he puffs like an
engine.)* Driver. You. Driver. I get it. You—driver. Easy.

GOCHER *laughs, the man laughs, then he holds his hand for silence again. He now makes his fingers into tight circles like spectacles and holds this before his eyes, looking wisely from side to side.* GOCHER watches intently.

TOVARISH.   Trot–sky.

Pause. The man stops the mime.

YOUNG GOCHER.   Trotsky.
Pause. The man does the train mime, with the guns, briefly, then the spectacles.

TOVARISH.   Trot—sky

Pause. GOCHER *is rigid with wonder.*

YOUNG GOCHER.   You—driver—you—*(The man stands rigidly to attention, making the red salute.)* Comrade Trotsky's engine driver. Comrade—Trotsky's—Fuck me! Fuck me! *(He forgets for a moment that he is chained.)* Bloody hell, comrade! Embrace me! Take me in yer arms, comrade! *(The man goes to him, arms outstretched. They clasp one another.* GOCHER *holds out the man's arms, peering at his large hands.)* What hands . . . what great big, wonderful hands . . . grabbing the levers . . . steering comrade Trotsky's train . . . faster, he says, more steam, more speed! Kick the English out of Mother Russia! And then these hands, these great big hands, transmit his message, down through the levers, down into the cogs and wheels . . . *(He gazes at the man's outspread hands for some moments. Suddenly,* STAVELEY *comes in.)*
STAVELEY.   Bloody cold. Persistently cold. Mercilessly, shatteringly cold! *(They both turn, look at him.)* Don't blame you for snuggling up. Got to end, though. Okay, Ivan? Up you get. Your own people, come to have a word with you. Out there. Waiting for you. Savvy? *(The man looks uncomprehendingly.)* Some of the Tsar's chaps. Through the door. *(He points. Slowly and fearfully, the man climbs off the bed, slowly makes his way out.)*
YOUNG GOCHER.   Ta, ta! See you later, Tovarish! *(He makes the red salute. The man, preoccupied, makes no response, goes out. Pause.)*
STAVELEY.   Shudderingly cruel, these people. Because they're Asiatics. In actual fact they aren't European at all. Not like us. No refinement. Everything about them, clothes for example, is a novelty. *(Pause.)* And with it, I'm afraid, an Asiatic appetite for slow death. A roaring imagination locked up in the contemplation of human pain. (GOCHER *looks at him suspiciously.)* I am personally of the opinion that pain is the dividing line between East and West. The attitude to it, I mean. Do you agree? *(*GOCHER *is silent.)* The abolition of pain simply does not seem a worthwhile object to them. I would go so far as to say that without it they would feel deprived. Whereas to us, that is the starting point of our national will, the common object of our efforts. *(Pause.)* I think the national characteristic is paramount in everything. I am certain that Russian socialism, just like Russian feudalism and Russian autocracy, will

always make us catch our breath. There is so much pain in them. Are you with me? *(Pause.)* Do you agree about the Russian character?

YOUNG COCHER *(confused but hostile).* You are after splittin' us! You are after driving a wedge into the international proletariat! I am not listening to you! *(He puts his hands over his ears. STAVELEY is unmoved.)*

STAVELEY. We are so alone. We are born alone, and we die alone. And there is nevery any contact. Isn't there enough agony for you?

YOUNG GOCHER. Christ, what's your game!

The doors fly open. The body of the engine driver is flung in. It rolls across the floor, stops in a heap. Pause.

STAVELEY. They have a place for you on a troopship. You are finished with Russia. *(He turns and walks smartly out.)*

Pause. GOCHER is gawping at the body of TOVARISH. He stretches as far as his chains will allow.

YOUNG GOCHER. Comrade . . . comrade . . . Tovarish . . . *(There is no movement.)* What happened, comrade? Oi, mate . . . ? *(Pause.)* Trotsky! Pro-le-tar-iat! *(Pause.)* Come on. Tovarish. Make a- *(Pause.)* I THINK HE'S DEAD! *(Pause. Then he yells, shaking his irons.)* You BASTARDS! Oi, you BASTARDS! Oi! Oi! Oi!

Blackout.

Scene Five

A spot near the parade ground designated as a cemetery. An empty stage but for a stretcher, on which the body of TOVARISH is lying. YOUNG GOCHER comes in, in an overcoat and woollen hat. He is carrying a shovel. He looks at the body for a few moments.

YOUNG GOCHER. I'm sorry, Tovarish, but it'll be a shallow one. Seeing as the ground is frozen. Six feet is a luxury out here. *(He flings the shovel into the ground, hacks at it. Stops.)* Did you have a name, I wonder? Because I'd like to drop a line to Comrade Trotsky about you. To tell him how you died. The heroic manner of your going. How at all times you upheld the honour of the proletariat. *(Pause.)* I think we can assume you did, which was why they had to murder you. Because you spat in their yellow eyes and told 'em how we were the workers of the world and how you had an English comrade in that very room. And that infuriated them, knowing how we were everywhere, joining hands across the language barrier. So they had to kill you, out of spite. They could not have heard History speaking in your mouth and let you live. *(Pause. He makes a few thrusts with the spade, stops again.)* The thing is, Tovarish old mate, the thing is, not how you live but how you serve. Which is why your life has not been wasted. Far from it. Your life—whole streets of people could not match that. You have been a world historical individual. *(Pause.)* Which I, at the moment, am not. I admit that. I have yet to make a contribution. I'd like to think I will be as world historical as you were. Though that's a lot to ask for. But it would please me, Christ, it would please me, because I do not want my life to be a nothing, a bit of flesh spewed up on the surface of the earth, a whining, giggling silver of biology. That is not enough for me. I state that now. Before your honoured body I swear the gift of life will not be chucked away by me! *(Long pause. Then he kneels beside the stretcher.)* The thing is, Tovarish, I have got to have you with me. I have got to have you guide me like you guided the great levers of his train. I am asking you to come to England with me, if you would. England, where Marx and Engels and Comrade Lenin sweated over books. Tovarish. I'm asking you to—

TOVARISH *(from the dead)*.   Kiev . . . my little garden in Kiev . . .

YOUNG GOCHER.   Kiev?

TOVARISH.   My allotment by the railway tracks . . .

YOUNG GOCHER.   I don't see what that has to do—

TOVARISH.   Who's going to dig my garden?

YOUNG GOCHER.   What I'm asking you, Tovarish, is would you mind—

TOVARISH.   WHO WILL DIG MY GARDEN! IT WILL GO TO SEED!

Pause.

YOUNG GOCHER.   Well, I . . . I don't . . .

TOVARISH.   MY DAHLIAS!

YOUNG GOCHER.   Christ, Tovarish . . .

TOVARISH.   KIDS WILL TRAMPLE ON MY DAHLIAS . . . !

YOUNG GOCHER.   Your hand . . . give me your hand . . . I only want your hand . . .

TOVARISH.   OH, MY POOR BLOODY DAHLIAS!

YOUNG GOCHER.   I want you hand! *(He quickly seizes the spade, and putting his foot on* TOVARISH's *wrist, brings the spade across it with a thud. Pause. He opens his eyes, slowly looks down, astonished.)* No blood . . .

He bends down, picks up the hand, gazes at it gingerly, then stuffs it in his great-coat pocket. STAVELEY *appears, carrying a small package beneath his arm.* GOCHER *begins digging with a vengeance.* STAVELEY *watches him from some yards away.*

STAVELEY.   Should someone say a prayer, do you think? (GOCHER *stops, looks at him.)* Quite happy to. *(Pause.)* Say what you like. (GOCHER *does not react.* STAVELEY *rummages in the packet and pulls out an icon.)* Hold this, you see. Over the body. *(Pause.)* To a dead Russian fellow . . .

Pause, then GOCHER *tackles the digging again, with desperation. Suddenly he flings down the shovel.*

YOUNG GOCHER.   I can't shift this fucking soil!

Pause.

STAVELEY.   Could do with a pick. Why don't you go and draw a pick? (GOCHER *looks at him.* STAVELEY *cleans the icon with his sleeve.*) Do you care for art? My wife loves it. Raves about it. Perfectly bonkers about art. Art's finished here, of course. No more art in Russia. Kaput!

YOUNG GOCHER.   They are gonna miss it.

STAVELY.   Art matters. Art does matter. *(He puts the icon back in the pocket.)*

YOUNG GOCHER.   Tell that to him.

STAVELEY.   You are so desperate, all you people. As if the world had only got ten minutes to live. It's very old, the world. It's a very old thing. If you want to know how old it is, look at the peasants. Peasants anywhere. They're all the same. You people should pay more attention to the peasants. Just look at them. See the accumulated wisdom in their eyes. They are nearer to the earth than you. And how still they are! I frequently think of peasants, and I always think of them as still . . .

YOUNG GOCHER.   They're ignorant. That's why they're still. They are stiff with bloody ignorance.

STAVELEY.   Of books. But not of the world, and they keep silence.

YOUNG GOCHER.   I will not listen to that! That is a lie! That is a lie to keep us down!

STAVELEY.   How quickly you sense a conspiracy. There is always a conspiracy in your eyes.

YOUNG GOCHER.   There is one! And the finding out of it is what hurts you.

STAVELEY.   No. What hurts me is that you have got your blood up and you will trample over everything. In pursuit of one blinding insight you will trample the whole garden of our culture.

YOUNG GOCHER.   Ours? Our culture? It's your culture. Not mine. I have no culture.

STAVELEY.   Share mine, then.

YOUNG GOCHER.   Some hope.

STAVELEY.   It's the pig trough without it. Gocher. It is the pig trough and the bear pit.

YOUNG GOCHER.   Don't give me that. I don't wanna hear all that. All your stuff. All your wisdom. Stuff it. Let me bury my dead mate. (He turns, picks up the shovel and attempts to hack at the ground. Pause.)

STAVELEY.   Off soon. Back to England.

YOUNG GOCHER.   So you said.

Long pause. GOCHER *digs.*

STAVELEY.   I want you to do something for me. Or more precisely, for my wife. (GOCHER *stops, leans on the shovel.*) I want you take a package to my wife.

YOUNG GOCHER.   A package . . .

STAVELEY.   Yes *(He holds out the package he has been carrying.)*

YOUNG GOCHER.   What's in it?

STAVELEY.   Icons. *(Pause.)* I am salvaging the icons.

YOUNG GOCHER.   But they're—

STAVELEY.   Sending 'em home.

Pause.

YOUNG GOCHER.   They don't belong to you.

STAVELEY.   They do. They belong to the world of art.

YOUNG GOCHER.   You're stealing 'em!

STAVELEY.   No. Saving them.

YOUNG GOCHER.   For who?

STAVELEY.   Man.

YOUNG GOCHER.   Man?

STAVELEY.   If they stay here the Bolsheviks will burn them. They burn
   everything.

YOUNG GOCHER.   Let 'em. Let 'em burn 'em.

STAVELEY.   I will not.

YOUNG GOCHER.   You're looting! That is a capital offence! That is a
   shooting offence, you bloody officer!

STAVELEY.   When you and your panic have died down, as you will, when
   your frenzy is forgotten, these icons will belong to Man. They are the
   legacy of the past to the present, and they actually matter more than you.
   They are Man in contemplation, in wisdom, serenity and repose, whereas
   you are Man in stinking sweat.

YOUNG GOCHER.   They are the people's property!

STAVELEY.   To burn.

YOUNG GOCHER.   To shit on, if they want to. To wipe their arses with!

STAVELEY.   You tartar. You sheer envy. You bloody, blind malice.

YOUNG GOCHER.   You thieving toff. (*Pause. They glare at one another,
   then* STAVELEY *turns on his heel and goes out.* GOCHER *watches him
   go, then takes out the severed hand.*) Tovarish! Against all their sodding
   culture I raise your hand, your working hand!

Blackout.

Scene Six

The Prison Hospital. GOCHER *is sitting up in bed. Beside him on an iron
locker, the bottled hand. Standing looking at him, a woman of about 30.*

MOIRA.   You old shit. You crazy old shit.

GOCHER (*with a shrug*).   Just an idea . . .

MOIRA.   You get me here. You cost me a train fare. You lose me one day's
   sodding earnings—

GOCHER.   I'll pay you.

MOIRA.   Yes, you will!

GOCHER.   I said I will.

MOIRA.   For what? To make a most disgusting proposition.

GOCHER.   Not disgusting.

MOIRA.   What else is it?

GOCHER. Not disgusting. All this clamour about sacred bodies, there is nothing sacred about bodies.

MOIRA. To have a man against my will.

GOCHER. All right. Does that hurt you?

MOIRA. Does it!

GOCHER. Doing a day's work is against your will. Half your bloody life carried on against your will. Why the issue over five minutes' worth of fanny? If you were starving it'd be the first thing you would barter.

MOIRA. My body is my property.

GOCHER. They've taught you that. They've taught you to make a fetish of your fanny, having nicked your labour from you.

MOIRA. It's what I feel!

GOCHER. They leave you that, to prize and perfume and offer very scrupulously. It's your one remaining property.

MOIRA. I don't know what you're on about.

GOCHER. Protect your brain! They have pinched your brain and you are on about your fanny, you poor bitch.

MOIRA. Oh, Christ, belt up, Dad!

GOCHER. HELP ME!

MOIRA. No! *(Pause.)* No. You are here because you did a murder and you ought to suffer for it. Seems only fair to me. *(Pause.)* I'm sorry, but that is justice. I think so, anyway. *(She walks a little way, stops.)* Anyway, supposing I did. Suppose I let him have me. How would that help? One warder? I'd have to have every feller between here and the main gate, wouldn't I? Then the last one would be queer. It's not on. It's a burkish idea. You're cracked.

Pause.

GOCHER. Try it.

MOIRA. Oh, fuck!

GOCHER. I ask nothing of you, do I? What have I asked? In ten years? Nothing. You have been a stranger to me. And now I ask one thing of you. To get me out. Do it. Sign off and shut the book. You won't hear no more of me. Nobody will.

She looks at him. Pause.

MOIRA. I was coming out of school at four o'clock, and this copper, jammed behind his steering wheel like a Christmas turkey in a gift box, window wound down, very casual, calls me over, with a little nod of his fat head, and asks me, have I got a father in an old folk's home? And I thought straight away, he's dead. I shall have to go to London. I didn't think, the poor old sod, he's kicked it, I thought I shall have to go to London, that is a drag. *(Pause. GOCHER does not react.)* And then he said—and this is what got me—he was grinning like he expected me to share the joke with him—he's gone and done a murder. Just like that, with all these kids from my class, standing round me open mouthed. Don't they teach them tact or anything? *(Pause.)* And then I thought, sod him. You, I mean. Let him stew.

Pause.

GOCHER.   Don't you love me any more?
MOIRA.   LOVE? Love YOU?
GOCHER.   Yes.
MOIRA.   Bloody hell. Bloody hell, Dad.
GOCHER.   Something, surely? Something tucked away?
MOIRA.   You bugger. You calculating bugger.

Pause. He shrugs, with embarrassment.

GOCHER.   Worth a try.
MOIRA.   You ask me that.
GOCHER.   Never mind.
MOIRA.   You, who put that object in the bottle before me at all times. You, who rammed your rubbish down my throat until I was screaming for the Empire Loyalists. You cranky, embarrassing old thing.
GOCHER.   All right. Sod off.
MOIRA.   That's more like it.
GOCHER.   SOD OFF!

LEARY *comes in, looking at his watch.*

LEARY.   That's it for today. Sorry. (*He walks round, swinging his whistle on a chain.* MOIRA *gathers herself to go.*) Toute suite back into the outside world, eh? Gasping up the oxygen? I've watched people put their arms round trees and kiss 'em after their first visit here.

Pause. She is about to go, but stops, looks at LEARY.

MOIRA.   You can have me if you want.
GOCHER *(horrified).*   Not like that!
LEARY *(who has stopped swinging his whistle).*   Sorry?
MOIRA.   I said you can have me if you want. (*Pause.* LEARY *gawps.*) Get it? (*He is speechless.* MOIRA *adjusts her shoulder bag, turns to* GOCHER.) No takers. Scheme falls flat.
GOCHER.   You silly cow.
MOIRA.   You said to offer. I am offering!
GOCHER.   Not like that!
LEARY.   What is this?
MOIRA.   It is a matter of principle with him that all coppers are corruptible. Like all the Left in England he under-estimates the opposition.
GOCHER.   Sabotaged it! My one get-out! Shit on it!
LEARY.   I think you're upsetting him.
MOIRA.   That's right.
GOCHER.   I am gonna die in here!
LEARY.   He's an old geezer. What's the point in upsetting him?
MOIRA.   It's called revenge.
LEARY.   I don't think I like it.
MOIRA.   Funny sentiment for a screw.

GOCHER.   Leave her. Leave her. There's no hope for her.

MOIRA.   That's right. I'm trapped in my historical condition. I'm to be pitied, really. I need help. *(She starts to go out, hesitates, stops.)* You look at him, and it could almost move you, couldn't it? But that's an old man's trick. He is steaming with violence. Throbbing with it, aren't you? Sweating and steaming under there . . .

Pause, then she goes out. LEARY *walks a little way, stops, looks at* GOCHER. *There is a moment of tacit intimacy.*

GOCHER.   You and me, Leary.

Pause.

LEARY.   Looks like it.

GOCHER.   No tricks now. No more gimmicks. No more cunt. Just what I tell you. Pure truth. A very fine oil, Leary, trickling down your earholes into yor stiff head, penetrating the clockwork of your indignation . . .

LEARY.   Good on yer, pop.

Pause.

GOCHER.   You are no gaoler, Leary. You are only in the clothes.

LEARY.   What am I, then?

GOCHER.   A man with a sense of Justice. Who thinks he finds it in a gaol. A man who thunders at the raping of a kiddie, but who has no satisfaction from shoving the perpetrator down the stairs. Am I right, Leary?

LEARY.   You *can* natter.

GOCHER.   Don't resist your own intelligence.

Pause.

LEARY.   And mind you don't flatter me. Mind you don't try too hard.

Pause, then he goes out. GOCHER *sits up alone for a good five seconds before the lights fade.*

Scene Seven

Brixton High Road, circa 1924. Standing on an empty stage, YOUNG GOCHER, *hands in pockets of a tatty demob suit. Beside him, on the floor, the bottled hand of* TOVARISH.

YOUNG GOCHER.   Home. Old England. The Brixton High Road, 1924. Waiting for the rising which must come. Says Lenin. Daily expectation in the Soviets. Meanwhile I am FUCKING STARVING! With my record no employer wants to look at me. Street corner layabout. Watching the traffic. Getting mesmerized. SNAP OUT OF IT! All right, but do what? Who am I? *(Pause.)* In Capitalist society a man is what he owns. A man is what he stands up in. *(Pause. He looks at himself, opens his jacket, looks at a mouldering shirt underneath. His eyes travel to his shoes, the soles of*

*which are flapping off. He walks a few paces, the soles flap noisily. He
stops, takes off a shoe, looks at it. He is barefoot. He shakes the shoe. It
flaps like a castanet. He removes the other shoe, and shakes them together.
They make a primitive rhythm. He starts to shake a tune on the shoes, then
stops, full of digust. He looks at the bottle, as if reproaching it.)* A man
must eat! First, he has to eat! *(He hesitates, as if embarrassed by the bottle,
but then, overcoming it, he bends down and rolls up his trousers as far as
they will go. Then he pulls his jacket up over his head, leaving it buttoned
and the sleeves empty. Finally, with a grimace, he starts slapping the shoes
together in a crude, tap-dancing manner, and performs a sand dance round
the bottle. He stops in a paroxysm of humiliation. Then he continues. An
occasional coin is flung on from the wings. Encouraged,* GOCHER
*performs with more polish. A few more pennies roll in. Taped laughter as
from a theatre queue. He dances on until he is too tired to continue. He sits
down wearily and begins collecting the money.)*

Enter unobserved, GOCHER's *former officer,* STAVELEY, *in evening
dress. He watches as* GOCHER *crawls around collecting up the pennies.
Casually, he lets a pound note flutter to the ground.* GOCHER *is about to
reach for it, looks up.*

STAVELEY. Got guts, Gocher. Got guts. *(Pause.* GOCHER *slowly
recognizes him.)* Got awful shellshock. After you left. Got banged on.
Buggered me. *(Pause. He manages to smile.* GOCHER *resting on his
knees, picks up the note, then pulls the coat up again, and starts another
performance. He is even better this time.* STAVELEY *watches.)* Needs a
song, though. Like everything nowadays. It needs a song. I said to
ladyfriend. 'What Gocher's lacking is a song. Said yes. Said altogether
hysterical, but needs a song. What do you say to a song? *(Pause.)* What do
you say? To a song?

Pause. GOCHER *stops performing.*

YOUNG GOCHER.   Since I saw you I have not earned one penny. In three
years. I have not earned a thing.
STAVELEY.   No. No, indeed.
YOUNG GOCHER.   Until this moment, when I made an idiot of myself.
When I pissed on myself, I made money.
STAVELEY.   Saw the moment. Grabbed it. What others pass by, you
seized on. Knew a chap. Made money. Know how? *(Pause.)* Bird shit.
Millionaire by bird shit. It is all round you. You don't see it. Then you
stoop, and there it is. Phelgm. Somebody will. Or starve.
YOUNG GOCHER.   And what are you?
STAVELEY.   Entertainment. Banish the gloom. Why the hand?
YOUNG GOCHER.   No reason.
STAVELEY.   They love it. They have really bought the hand. Just the song
that's missing. Will you try? Love to help you.
YOUNG GOCHER.   Help me?
STAVELEY.   Help you. *(Pause.)* What's happened's happened. Strange
circumstances. World hiccupped and we all got burped. Bit of acid came
up. All right now.

YOUNG GOCHER.   Not all right now.

STAVELEY.   The heart beat. The heart beat is humanity. The belching is politics. My opinion, naturally.

YOUNG GOCHER.   I don't share your opinion.

STAVELEY.   Why should you. All opinions, only wavelets, but the river carries on.

YOUNG GOCHER.   I do not have that view! That view of things, it is pure poison to me!

STAVELEY. Okay.

YOUNG GOCHER.   It is not okay! I am what I am, and you are what you are, and I am what I am because of you. So it is not okay, is it? It is not okay.

Pause.

STAVELEY.   Sing about it. Sing about your condition, then.

Pause. GOCHER *glares at him.*

YOUNG GOCHER.   Christ, I had a rifle once. And I let them take it off of me . . .

Pause. STAVELEY *takes out a card, slips it in* GOCHER's *top pocket.*

STAVELEY.   When you want me, that's where I am.

He goes out. GOCHER *sits wearily down, looks at the bottle. Pause.*

YOUNG GOCHER.   The first thing, Tovarish, the first thing is that this is not your homeland. The circumstances while being international in character, are not identical. I am angry. I am angry but that doesn't seem to be enough. ANGER IS NOT EDIBLE! *(Pause.)* I am inclined to compose a song, I admit that. Though it degrades me, am I not equally degraded by starvation? Yes, I am. And also, I might add, ridiculing myself in the theatre queue is no greater a humiliation than that experienced daily by our working people. So in a sense, it is an act of solidarity I am performing. Arguably. *(Pause.)* Do you agree? *(Pause.)* I would appreciate your agreement because I am very near to having composed a song. I need your blessing, Tovarish! *(Pause.)* Thank you. *(Pause, then he gets up, and by an act of sheer willpower, divests himself of the song, tapping the shoes all the while and dancing.)*

I'm out of a job, I'm out of my shoes, I say to Mr. Moon, I'm spending the night at the Park Bench Suite, Don't wake me up till noon! *(He performs a chorus with the shoes.)* Ach—cha—cha—Ach—cha; cha—Ach— cha; cha—Ach—Chaka—Chaka—ta, Cha, cha! *(He stops, long pause.)*

Fade to black.

Scene Eight

Wandsworth Prison Hospital. GOCHER *is sitting up in bed.* LEARY *is sitting on a chair, tipping it on to its back legs, hands in pockets.*

GOCHER.   You must have thought of murder.

LEARY.   On and off.

GOCHER.   Real murder?

LEARY.   Sometimes I am crawling with it. But I have never done it. Or many acts of violence, for that matter.

GOCHER.   Well, I did. In cold blood. In the dead of night, in all the whistling and snoring of old men. While the night nurse read his paperback. Down on the little white skull, which gave way like egg. Caved in, like egg.

LEARY.   Who was he?

GOCHER.   A Pole. A Catholic Pole.

LEARY.   Do you hate Poles?

GOCHER.   He was my first and last Pole. I had asked him a good route to Russia, and he took against me, being a Pole. Screeching about what the Red Army had done to his sister in the 20s. How they had shot her, because she was a nun. And his estate, how they had quartered Mongols on it. Etcetera. Until he was sedated. And all this balls about the Vatican. There was a gulf between us.

LEARY.   So you bashed him.

GOCHER.   He threatened me. He was going to give away my secret. I had no option but to bash him.

LEARY.   You and your secret.

GOCHER.   My secret, Leary. Which is down to you, now.

LEARY.   Ever hopeful . . . *(He gets up.)*

GOCHER.   Hopeful, yes! You make it sound like a weakness, that I have hope in you, Christ, we are fucking maggots without hope!

LEARY.   And silly bastards with it.

GOCHER.   Leary, you could lift me out of here. Under yer raincoat. I'm as light as a feather . . .

LEARY.   I am paid to keep blokes in, not smuggle 'em out.

GOCHER.   That's not a life. That is pissing on life. That is standing on the edge of a shit pan, poking geezers under with a stick. Is that your life's work, Leary? Jesus Christ.

LEARY.   They call it duty. Have you ever heard of it?

GOCHER.   That's right. It's the name they give to every function that a normal human being would spew on.

LEARY.   Got all the answers, grandad, haven't you? Book of Knowledge. Tree of Life.

GOCHER.   Get us to the Steppes, Leary! Let the Siberian winds blow through yer brain. This country, this fuddling country, stuffing cotton wool up every orifice, you can't breathe here, you can't smell or taste here, it is cotton wool!

Pause.

LEARY. This is the hospital, pop. I suggest you make the most of it.
GOCHER. I'm right, I'm right, can't you see I'm fucking right!

LEARY looks at him. GOCHER, exhausted, lies back asleep on his pillow. Pause, then LEARY turns to go out. Blackout.

Scene Nine

Roar of applause, as in a theatre. Sound of a banjo being strummed. YOUNG GOCHER, *with characteristic shuffle, enters in his legendary costume, flapping soles on his shoes, trousers rolled up high, coat over head. Applause increases in volume. He begins singing, accompanying himself on the banjo.*

YOUNG GOCHER. I am a no—bo—dy, No—bo—dy care for me,
  Ain't got a job, Ain't got no wife, no responsibility!
  I takes a stroll a—round,
  Like a real toff on the town,
  Sometimes I laughs, sometimes I cries,
  Sometimes I feel right down.
  The copper says to me,
  The deckchairs are not free,
  Get off your bum, Move on now, son,
  You're a—*(pretending to stifle a swear word)* Lia—bil—ity!

Big roar of applause. With a grin, GOCHER *performs a tap-dance with his shoes, and then shuffles off. Final roar, which cuts off suddenly. He comes back in, loosening the jacket over his head. Spot on* GOCHER, *in bed.*

GOCHER. Every voice lifted in song was one less calling for the revolution. Every hand clap was a clap for putting up with it. And putting up with it. And putting up with it . . .
YOUNG GOCHER *(his eyes closed).* I know . . . I know . . .
GOCHER. All their hot blood, all their outrage, lost in your racket.
YOUNG GOCHER. I did ask Tovarish. I asked him—
GOCHER. In front of them! On the stage in front of them, the hand, the subject of a ghastly comedy. A trademark for a sellout!
YOUNG GOCHER *(turning on him).* Easy, when you've spent years in bed! Seeing where you went wrong from the clean sheets! What can't be solved from a bedroom, with yer meals brought to you on a tray! There is no philosophy where there is no food. Right, Tovarish? *(He looks at the bottle.)* Yes, right! *(Pause. He looks down at the floor.)* You know what I mean . . . I hid nothing from myself. But they were not ready. Looking in their faces, I could see they were nowhere near ready.

Fade to black on YOUNG GOCHER, *lights up on* OLD GOCHER. *A young* DOCTOR *comes in, carrying a stethoscope and bag. As he talks, he puts the bag down on a chair, takes out a thermometer, shakes it, puts it in* GOCHER's *mouth, then takes his pulse.*

DOCTOR. Played a banjo, did he? In the thirties? George Formby sort of thing? Made records? Never heard of him. Must have been hundreds in his day. Like pop stars now. They come and go. One hit and then forgotten. Buried. Bus drivers now, who once had strummed the Fender and sent tingles through the bowels of little girls. Gas fitters, who once had made the front seats of the Odeon sop with the piss of juvenile incontinence. Open the gob. Not dead, are we? Be good. Open thy trap. Don't tease. Say Ah. Say Ah. Ah—ah! (GOCHER *opens his mouth.*) Oh, ugly is the cakehole! Any pain?

GOCHER. YES, PAIN!

DOCTOR. Description. Can you manage a description?

GOCHER. MISERY!

DOCTOR. The lungs? The lungs is it? I read somewhere.

GOCHER. Let an old man out of here.

DOCTOR. Would do. Like a shot would do. Breathe deep. Breathe deep. Then out. *(He bends to place the stethoscope against* GOCHER's *scrawny chest.)* Hear the rattling bronchioles, the trachae in their squealing choruses. Does that hurt?

Suddenly, reaching for the bottled hand on the locker, GOCHER *brings it down squarely on the* DOCTOR's *head. The* DOCTOR *sinks slowly to the floor.*

GOCHER. Christ, Tovarish, could have shattered yer . . . *(He looks at the bottle anxiously, then mustering all his energy, swings himself round and sits on the side of the bed.)* No power in me pins, now. I have wasted in this sodding bed. And all Europe to cross! *(He kneels down and starts removing the* DOCTOR's *white overall.)* France, Germany, Belgium, Poland . . . an old bloke slipping by their frontier posts . . . a dark speck crawling on the map . . . *(He puts on the coat, over his pyjamas.)* Gocher, your lonely travel through the world . . . you epic old bugger, you! *(He grins to himself, picks up the* DOCTOR's *bag and turns to go out. As he does so,* LEARY *appears.* GOCHER *freezes,* LEARY *folds his arms. Pause, then* GOCHER *sits wearily on the bed.)* Couldn't have done it, anyway . . .

Pause.

LEARY. Neversawyer. (GOCHER *looks up, puzzled.*) Neversawyer. (GOCHER *is gawping. Pause.*) Don't hang about!

GOCHER. What . . . What . . . What . . . *(Pause.)* What are you saying?

LEARY. I'm not saying anything. And I'm not seeing anything either.

GOCHER. You are up to something! You have got a scheme!

LEARY. He will come round in a minute. Or you have killed him.

GOCHER. You're after something, Leary—

LEARY. He's moving . . . Look at him . . .

GOCHER. You'll let me get to the bloody main gate and you'll squeal on me!

LEARY.   CHRIST! JESUS CHRIST! You tell me what it is to be a man. You talk about intelligence and goodness and what goodness I have got in me. And when I show it, you have NO FAITH.

Long pause.

GOCHER.   Come with us.
LEARY.   What for? You need an arm to lean on?
GOCHER.   Come with us. *(Pause.)* You'll get old in this place. Moss will grow along yer spine . . . *(Pause.)* There's nothing for you here. Escape, Leary . . .

Pause. LEARY looks at GOCHER for several seconds. Then the DOCTOR emits a groan. LEARY turns, looks at him. GOCHER holds out the bottle. Pause. LEARY takes the bottle, goes to the DOCTOR and strikes him. They look at one another. Fade to black.

Scene Ten

A plain desk and chair, as in a classroom. Seated at the desk, MOIRA.

MOIRA.   Confessions. What I did. At Training College. *(Pause.)* Went out with policemen. More than one. I was very keen on policemen at the time. I think any policeman could have had me, I was that keen on them. I was blind. Men in blue shirts even had a pull for me. *(Pause.)* And this one who I loved—I did love him, get that straight—said who are all the militants? In bed one night. Who are all the militants? And I named them. Which he took down with a pencil. He was never at a loss for a pencil. Even naked he could lay hands on a pencil. And because he was so pleased with me, I kept on doing it. I got a real thrill out of it. All these characters I'd never liked, down in his book, being typed up, going in the records, filed in cabinets. All on my say so. All the people I had hated, all the shouters, down for good. *(Pause.)* And then I was a teacher. All these rows of little heads. Not teenage fuck and scuffle, but big eyes you can shove ideas through. And I did. Jesus and Solzhenitsyn, the two big gentle people from the East. I had them squealing like a pack of Pavlov's dogs at strikers or trade unions. And why not? After what he'd done to me, with his whining at SOCIETY. I was sick of the word SOCIETY, it was hanging on his lips like a wet fagend what was happening in SOCIETY. I thought you ignorant old sod, consumed with jealousy, you have no education, all you've got is bitterness, you are sopping with it like an old incontinent. *(Pause.)* But having seen him, I think he has licked himself. He has been chewed up and spat out for it. I have discovered what I thought his barminess had extinguished in me. I feel pity. Outside the place, looking back at all the little windows, I thought that thing you've left in there, that skin and bone thing, is your DAD. *(Pause.)* And I was touched. Amazing.

Pause. Then a siren goes off. Blackout.

Scene Eleven

Wandsworth Common. On a bare stage, LEARY *still in warder's uniform, but without the hat, and the tunic undone, is helping* GOCHER *along.* GOCHER *still wears the* DOCTOR's *coat over his pyjamas. He clutches the bottle.*

GOCHER.   I can't keep up! How can I keep up! Let a bloke rest, will yer?

LEARY.   They'll be chucking cordons around the place. They'll have road blocks up.

GOCHER.   Where are we? How far have we got?

LEARY.   The Common. I can still see the main gate if I look.

GOCHER.   We have come miles!

LEARY.   A yard's a mile the way you move.

GOCHER.   Christ, and I am dropping.

LEARY.   You can't drop.

GOCHER.   I am a sodding old age pensioner!

LEARY.   You can't break out of prison and then drop. Not in sight of the main gate. I'll carry you.

GOCHER.   Let's rest. Let's have a rest. *(He sits on the ground.)*

LEARY.   We don't half look conspicuous. In a white coat in the middle of a common. Bloody conspicuous.

GOCHER.   You're all nerves.

LEARY.   What's a long sentence to you? It's nothing to an old bloke. I will lose my best years. They are sheer bloody sadists when it comes to dealing with bent screws.

GOCHER.   I can't move. I can't move yet!

LEARY.   That's dogs! I can hear dogs!

Pause.

GOCHER.   Can't hear nothing—

LEARY *silences him with a movement of his hand. They listen rigidly.*

LEARY.   No trouble following our scent. The way you stink.

GOCHER.   I'm old.

LEARY.   Do old men have to stink? Is it biological?

GOCHER.   I happens.

LEARY.   Why?

GOCHER.   Yer don't polish a rotten apple.

LEARY.   Pity. As I've got to carry you.

GOCHER.   Spray us with something.

LEARY.   When we get near Woolworths. Douse you in hair lacquer. *(Suddenly he gets to his feet.)* That's dogs! Get up!

GOCHER.   I will never like dogs. They will lick the hands of mass murderers.

LEARY.   So will people. And they are mass murderers. *(He drags* GOCHER *to his feet.)* Get up. Get on my back. *(He kneels.* GOCHER *feebly tries to climb on.)* Jesus . . .

GOCHER. I can't do it . . .
LEARY. Get on! Get on my back!
GOCHER. I've got a pain . . .
LEARY. Sod it, get on my back!
GOCHER. You'll have to leave me, Leary—
LEARY. GET ON!
GOCHER. Oh, Christ . . .
LEARY. I can't stop now. However much it hurts you. Can't stop now.
GOCHER. LEA—RY!

Clutching GOCHER *as best he can,* LEARY *runs off stage. As he does so, stage staff drag on from the other side of a railway platform seat with the legend 'Wandsworth Common' fixed to it. Tape of a train receding.* LEARY *enters wearily with* GOCHER *still clinging to his back.*

LEARY. Missed it. We have missed it. *(Pause.)* Christ. *(He looks into the distance until the sound stops.)* Get down, then. Grandad. Off you get. (GOCHER *is sagging, his hand still rigidly round the bottle, but his eyes are closed.)* Come on! *(As* GOCHER *appears unable to hear or move,* LEARY *has to disengage himself. He kneels, crawls out, supports* GOCHER *into the platform seat. As the old man's head lolls backwards,* LEARY *takes his jacket off, rolls it up, places it under his head. He then sits himself, exhausted. Pause.)* What am I doing? What am I doing? *(Pause.)* LEARY, YOU ARE FUCKING MAD! *(Pause.)* You, who were so certain where you stood. In fifteen minutes you have turned into cellfodder! *(Pause. He looks sideways at* GOCHER.*)* Leave him. What I should do. Leave him *(He stands up. Pause.)* LEAVE HIM! *(He closes his eyes, grits his teeth, then angrily sits again.)* I have been corrupted by pity! Pity is destroying me!
GOCHER *(suddenly bursting out, his head still drooping back).*
  I met this young lady, I rang at her bell,
  I said I've been tramping, I'm thirsty as hell,
  She gave me one look and said come on right in,
  For a man with your needs I've got just the thing!

Lights flick out.

Scene Twelve

A dressing-room at the Hammersmith Empire, 1935. A table with a mirror, two chairs. YOUNG GOCHER, *in a professional tramp's costume, and heavily made up, is sprawled in a chair looking at himself distantly in the mirror. Some way away, pensively watching him, a woman of about 30.*

YOUNG GOCHER. Hammersmith Empire. Top of the Bill. 1935. A full house haemorrhaging itself with encores. Roaring as I do my beggar's shuffle. Working men . . . *(Pause.)* I felt like . . . what I always feel like . . . that I should have . . . stopped and said . . . *(Pause. He picks up his banjo, adapts his funny posture and starts strumming and shuffling.)*

I was sayin' to the missus you can pawn the cat,
You can pawn me medals, me braces or me hat,
But I don't care how much dough we owe,
You're never gonna pawn me ol' banjo!

(Suddenly he brings the banjo down onto the floor with a tremendous smash. Pause. He looks into the audience.) I have shit on you. You have paid to come here, and I have shit on you. No, don't laugh missus, I'm not ill. Stop smiling, it's not funny. It's a fucking tragedy. You and your wonderful good humour, your British talent for seeing it through. CHRIST! You would have your daughters in the brothel and still not lift a finger! I tell you it's not funny! It is not funny that we are here to laugh at our communal bloody misery, it is a sin! Don't you understand what I have done to you, you ragged arsed workers! Have some pity on yourselves, have some pride and pity for your own sakes! *(Pause. He goes back, sits in the chair.)* Something like that. If I said anything.

Pause.

MELANIE. They'd pee in their caps and sling it at you.
YOUNG GOCHER. All right! But in the street, as they walked home, they would be silent. It would sink in.
MELANIE. Some hope.
YOUNG GOCHER. Well, what then!
MELANIE. You can't give people what they don't want. They will find it, when they want it.
YOUNG GOCHER. What do you have to do to them? To move them? What do you prick their arses with?
MELANIE. You talk like that. The way you talk. You are an arrogant bugger.
YOUNG GOCHER. Not arrogant. Got eyes. Since when was it arrogant to use your eyes?
MELANIE. You have no right.
YOUNG GOCHER. I have the right! Any man who has a vision has the the right. Lenin had no right to kick the slob Kerensky, but he did it. There is too much chatter about rights. Always other people's rights. What about my rights? I claim the right, and balls to lawyers and professors and their sticky constitutions.

Pause.

MELANIE. You scare me. You do. You scare me.
YOUNG GOCHER. You don't want to be frightened of a banjo player.
MELANIE. Because I think there's nothing that you wouldn't do.

Pause.

YOUNG GOCHER. Lock the door, I'll show you.

MELANIE. No.
YOUNG GOCHER. I am sick minded and arrogant. And I fancy you.
MELANIE. No.
YOUNG GOCHER. Why not?
MELANIE. Because you're angry. I don't want you when you're angry.
YOUNG GOCHER. Christ, why not!
MELANIE. I'm not a thing to be shoved up against!

Long pause.

YOUNG GOCHER. Sometimes I have thought about my funeral. And it
has been a very big affair . . .

They looks at each other a moment.
Enter STAVELEY. *He sees the broke banjo.*

STAVELEY. Bust your banjo . . .
YOUNG GOCHER. Didn't know you were in tonight. *(He begins cleaning*
off his make-up.)
STAVELEY. Bust it . . . *(He looks at* MELANIE.) Bust his banjo . . .
YOUNG GOCHER. All right, Mr Staveley, I bust my banjo! *(Pause. He*
wipes his face.)
STAVELEY. Bust it again.
YOUNG GOCHER. What for?
STAVELEY. On stage. Bust it on stage.

GOCHER *looks confused.*

YOUNG GOCHER. Why, Mr Staveley?
STAVELEY. The act. The act, good as it is, would benefit. Would do
wonders from a little fracas. At the end of it. (GOCHER *is still*
incredulous.) A gag. A closer. Knock George Formby for a six. Later on
maybe, set light to it. Every night you bust it. Get it?
YOUNG GOCHER. Oh Christ, what this man will put his mind to!
(STAVELEY *looks injured.*) How you shit on your intelligence . . .
STAVELEY. I am sorry. I am sorry I make suggestions that will benefit
your career.
YOUNG GOCHER. CAREER! He calls this INDECENCY a CAREER!
(Pause.) Christ, how this country brings the vomit out in us . . .

Pause.

STAVELEY. You'd have been happier in Russia, I suppose. In a salt-mine.
Under whips.
MELANIE. Leave him, Mr Staveley . . .
STAVELEY. No, I won't just leave him. I have left him. I am always
leaving him. He is a myth-maker. He hates the people who pay to see him.
He despises the audience who love him, and I think that's vile. I think that
is a disgusting attitude for an entertainer to adopt. He has a private loyalty
to a society which would have eradicated him and his profession long ago,
a society where violence and killing have replaced any proper form of
government, where free debate has been suppressed and bureaucratic
savegery is the order of the day.

MELANIE.   Leave him. Leave off.
STAVELEY.   He is in love with a society that has denigrated civilization
and squandered common decency—
YOUNG GOCHER.   I WILL STRANGLE YOU.
STAVELEY.   Russia is a stinking place!
YOUNG GOCHER.   Get him out or I will strangle him!
STAVELEY.   Decent people pay to see you, you traitor! You moral cheat!

GOCHER *suddenly leaps to his feet and grabs* STAVELEY *by the throat.*

MELANIE. Get off him! (STAVELEY *is slowly throttled.*) Albert! Get off
him! GOD!

Slowly GOCHER *reduces* STAVELEY *to the floor, then lets him go.*

YOUNG GOCHER.   Did he think I'd argue with him? *(He goes to the table,
where the bottled hand is standing.)* When argument is so precious? Waste
it on him?
STAVELEY.   You—are—finished—Gocher . . . (GOCHER *ignores him,
looks at* TOVARISH's *hand.*) You—are—done—DONE!

Pause. MELANIE *looks desperately at them.*

MELANIE.   Make it up. Come on. Make it up.
STAVELEY *(rubbing his throat).*   I have lived among madmen. I have slept
in wards where men screamed every second of their sleep. Officers. War
heroes. Shuddering like tripe. I have witnessed every kind of madness but
there is no madness like RED MADNESS. God save our people and our
homes!
MELANIE.   He gets like that sometimes. Goes right off. Then he's all right.
Nice as anything.
STAVELEY.   He wants blood. It's blood he wants.
MELANIE.   Get you a cup of tea, shall I?
STAVELEY.   Blood and more blood.
MELANIE.   Tea. For your throat.
STAVELEY.   NOT LISTENING!

Pause. GOCHER *is examining the bottled hand.*

MELANIE.   Oh, he *has* marked you . . . oh, nasty . . .
STAVELEY.   NOT LISTENING!

Pause. GOCHER *turns.*

YOUNG GOCHER.   I have finished with it, Staveley. I don't play the
clown act any more.
STAVELEY.   No more.
YOUNG GOCHER.   I won't whistle the workers' minds away. For you.
STAVELEY.   No. Better work them up in some factory.
YOUNG GOCHER.   Yes.
STAVELEY.   Get them sweating.
YOUNG GOCHER.   Yes.

STAVELEY.   Get them frothing.

YOUNG GOCHER.   Yes.

MELANIE.   You are both being *so* silly. If only you could hear yourselves! Like a pair of tomcats hissing at each other. You really are! It's comical. I mean it would be if it wasn't so NASTY. Shake hands. *(Pause.)* Boys! *(Pause.)* Look, this is a bloody good act!

YOUNG GOCHER.   Other mugs where I come from.

MELANIE.   I LIKE THIS LIFE. *(Pause. She cannot believe it.)* Bertie. We have come from nowhere. We will end up nowhere. Do you like nowhere 'cos I don't!

STAVELEY.   It's what he wants. Success embarrasses him.

MELANIE.   We are doing so well, Gocher, we are BIG!

YOUNG GOCHER.   I hate talking in front of him. So I will keep it brief. I will say just this. There are times for action, and times for entertainment. And there are times when entertainment is a crime. THIS IS ONE OF THEM.

STAVELEY.   And you drag her down with you. Most considerate. You emboil her in your private vendetta. You gentleman.

YOUNG GOCHER *(picking up the bottle)*.   We're off.

MELANIE.   All right, but you haven't talked.

YOUNG GOCHER.   We have talked!

MELANIE.   Yeah, you've gone on at one another but you haven't talked. You haven't made it up, I mean.

YOUNG GOCHER.   COME ON.

MELANIE *(to STAVELEY)*.   Bertie has this view of things . . . this attitude he picked up . . . and sort of . . . it has sort of stuck with him . . . and now and then it comes out . . . big . . . you know . . . but really . . . it gets up people's noses but once you get to know him he—

YOUNG GOCHER.   Stop that.

MELANIE.   He's absolutely harmless and—

YOUNG GOCHER.   STOP THAT!

Pause.

STAVELEY.   You are very gentle. And very wise. I wish you well.

Pause.

MELANIE.   THIS IS ABSURD!

Pause. GOCHER goes out. MELANIE wants to say more to STAVELEY, but has to follow him. Pause. STAVELEY lights a cigarette, sits at the dressing-table, looks at his neck, relaxed. Pause.

STAVELEY.   I believe, you see—I believe that pain is vile. That PAIN is VILE. And in England there is not all that much pain. I would put up with any amount of trivia . . . any degree of ephemeral, piddling trivia . . . any degree of bungling incompetence and amateurishness . . . if we as a nation miss the PAIN. *(He gets up, picks up the broken banjo, looks at it. Pause.)* Catch on with somebody . . .

Blackout.

Scene Thirteen

Wandsworth Common Railway Station. LEARY and GOCHER are sitting on the bench. Staring at them from some distance away, a RAILWAY PORTER with a broom. He is immobile, suspicious. GOCHER has his eyes closed. LEARY, though aware of the PORTER does not look at him.

LEARY.   Don't give us away, you bugger. Don't go running to your telephone. Or I will have you. *(Pause. He looks up at the PORTER.)* All right?

The man nods, simply. GOCHER, lolling slightly, comes round, his gaze alights on the PORTER.

GOCHER.   Where's this? Germany?

LEARY *(looks at GOCHER for some seconds, then tentatively)*.   Yeah...

GOCHER.   I was in Germany. After the armistice. They marched us into Germany. You never saw starvation like it. Calcutta—nothing. *(He looks at the PORTER, extends a hand.)* I'm sorry, mate. *(The PORTER just looks.)* Kamerad...1918...me...*(He taps his chest.)* Me...Kamerad... Enschuldigen Sie . . . for the war . . . Das Kapitalism did it. Not me *(The PORTER looks at LEARY, who nods his head for the man to take GOCHER's hand. He takes it.)* The blockade . . . starved the little kiddies . . . but not me . . . *(Pause. GOCHER looks at LEARY.)* He don't say much.

LEARY.   He's overcome.

GOCHER.   No. He resents me. He remembers the blockade. *(He turns to the PORTER again.)* It's not the soldiers, mate. Never the soldiers. Nicht die Soldaten. Nicht. Nicht. Nicht. *(The   PORTER, still holding GOCHER's hand, nods his head.)* We let ourselves be robbed, eh, Kamerad? Took away our brains, filled us up with sawdust. Dumkopfs we were in our trenches, eh? Dumkopfs versus Dumkopfs? *(The PORTER just looks, GOCHER turns back to LEARY.)* He don't speak. Why don't he speak?

LEARY.   Moved. He's too moved.

GOCHER *(beckons the PORTER closer. Gingerly, the man leans near)*. Ich liebe dich. Ja? *(The PORTER nods.)* They taught us that to say to girls. But it suits. Ich liebe dich.

They grin at one another for a few moments, then the PORTER edges warily away.

LEARY.   Where are all the bloody trains?

GOCHER.   You can tell we are in Europe. The great blood bowl. Can't you smell it? Christ, the blood . . . the whole place is on a great seepage of blood. Under the grass, under the pavement. Dig down, and up it comes, bubbling through the clay!

LEARY *(getting up)*.   Murmansk we want, is it? Two singles to Murmansk?

GOCHER.   I was not shot, but I still suffered, Leary. No one knows the sufferings of an English idealist.

LEARY.   I'll get the tickets. Won't be long.

GOCHER.   I used to wonder when I heard of shootings, what if it was me, how would I feel? If I was standing there, in the cellar, against stone walls.

LEARY.   Not very pleasant, I imagine.

GOCHER.   On the contrary. You would have mattered. History would have laid her finger on you, or else why would you be there? What is your litle life, compared with the significance of being executed? It's your badge. It's your certificate of world historicalness, Leary. *(Pause.)* I have lost no blood. No one has sought me out in a cellar, or stopped me on a country road . . .

LEARY.   Until today. They are all after you today. *(He goes out.)*

GOCHER.   All my juices, spent in that dry soil . . .

Pause and blackout.

Scene Fourteen

Spotlight on YOUNG GOCHER, *in overalls, standing on a wooden crate. Pause. He mentally prepares.*

YOUNG GOCHER.   Comrades . . . *(He strokes his lip.)* Comrades . . . *(Pause.)* The class war is suspended. The patriotic war has begun. *(Pause.)* Yesterday I urged you—break the machines. Yesterday I said—cut through the driving belts, neglect the oilcan, loosen bolts. Yesterday I said—produce only when every obstacle to production is exhausted. Today I say to you—step up the power, sacrifice your teabreak, take time off only when your bladder or your bowels compel you to. Today I say— break records. *(Pause.)* Now why, comrades? Why this apparent about-face? Because you see, I hear you murmuring, I hear your rumbling doubts and queries. Is the boss the enemy, or is he not? *(Pause.)* To which I say, if only life were that simple! Because if life were that simple, we would have been the masters long ago. (Pause.) We are inspired by an ideal, an ideal which became reality, an ideal which has shifted the dead weight of history. The ideal of the Soviet Union. But while we are inspired by an ideal, our business is with facts. And today, with one fact in particular. Comrade Stalin, far away in his Kremlin, has especially asked me to acquaint you with this fact. And the fact is, that the Soviet Union has been attacked. *(Pause.)* Now, you do not need me to underline the meaning of that fact. Russia is attacked, the international working class movement is attacked, we are all attacked. *(Pause.)* So we suspend our conflict, our national conflict, in the wider interests of the world socialist movement. We close ranks with the capitalists not out of treason, but from loyalty—loyalty to the International working class. We work our fingers to the bone to defend the citadel of socialism and we discover a new slogan—NO SLACKING IN THE SOCIALIST STRUGGLE! Comrades, to your benches, to your lathes! *(Pause.)* Address to the Extraordinary General Meeting of the Shop Stewards' Committee of the Engineering Union, the Borough, July, 1941.

A second SPOT flicks on to MELANIE, *pregnant.*

MELANIE.   Bertie Gocher, what about me!

YOUNG GOCHER.   Get work, Melanie.

MELANIE.   Get work?

YOUNG GOCHER.   War work. Get in munitions, ship-building. And no striking!

MELANIE.   If you had stuck with entertainment I would never needed to have worked.

YOUNG GOCHER.   Don't dig up the past, please.

MELANIE.   I am not a communist! And I'm not a Russian! All this time you put in for the Russians!

YOUNG GOCHER.   I have explained to the meeting it is not for the Russians. That is a petty-bourgeois xenophobic statement. Please retract it.

MELANIE.   Russia matters more than me!

YOUNG GOCHER.   That is an uninformed attitude. You are confusing the personal with the political.

MELANIE.   I am saying that it matters more than me! Deny it.

YOUNG GOCHER.   I cannot deny a figment of your imagination.

MELANIE.   Sod it, Gocher, sod it!

YOUNG GOCHER.   Please, this is silly, isn't it?

MELANIE.   Silly or not I want it answered. Do you love Russia more than me?

Pause.

YOUNG GOCHER.   It is not a relevant—

MELANIE.   Re-phrase it. You. For the benefit of. If you had to choose between—if it was in your power—silly I know—but got to answer—speak or die—whether Russia carried on or not—and me—which would it be—reply.

YOUNG GOCHER.   This simply does not matter.

MELANIE.   Answer! Or I will do this—thing—in me an injury.
(Pause. He looks at her, shocked.) Because I am determined to hear you give an honest answer. I am nothing. I know that. I am uneducated. I am shit. I could learn but I have turned my back on it. Other wives are communists and very happy, but me, no. Bask in my ignorance. Deeply shocking waste of human potential. Poor contrast with Soviet womanhood, I know. But answer me, Gocher. I want an answer now. Say it!

Pause.

YOUNG GOCHER.   Russia, of course.

Pause.

MELANIE.   This is your kid. Nobody else's. And when I've had it, I am giving it to you, and I'm going away. I have scarcely seen you, so you won't be missed. And vice-versa, I expect.

YOUNG GOCHER. Melanie, I have an ideal, and I am not ashamed of it. Men are nothing without ideals.

MELANIE. That? What you have? That an ideal? Comrade bloody Stalin an ideal?

YOUNG GOCHER. Changing history! Putting your foot out and tripping up history, that's my ideal! *(Pause.)* And you should have an ideal. You do yourself an injury by leaning on a man. As if without him you are nothing. You are something. On your own.

MELANIE. Don't worry. I am on my own all right. Only the ideal of being your housekeeper and kids' nurse somehow doesn't appeal to me. I wonder why. I can get by without ideals. They have poisoned you, Gocher. They have brought you down.

Pause.

YOUNG GOCHER. I love you.

Pause.

MELANIE. Christ . . .

YOUNG GOCHER. I shouldn't have to keep on saying that . . .

MELANIE *(looks at him, shaking her head).* Christ . . . what a way with words he has . . . what a magician . . . as if that little phrase would tie me down. You eternal bloody optimist.

YOUNG GOCHER. Blimey! And there are Russian women, and there are German women for that matter, walking with pistols at their sides! *(He shakes his head.)* It makes you think . . . while we squabble, what they do . . .

MELANIE. Don't insult us. You people, always bringing up your foreigners to fling at us, to measure us by. (GOCHER *closes his eyes in despair.*) I will have the child, and tell you where you can collect it. Then I'm going north, to Scotland. I'm going away from the war as far as I can go. And if the Germans win it, I will be married to a German, I expect. If he'll have me. And all over Russia there are women just the same.

Pause.

YOUNG GOCHER. You fill me with despair.

MELANIE. I do. I know I do. I bring you down.

YOUNG GOCHER. With your persistent pessimism, your pseudo-realism. You make human weakness a subject for vanity. And I can't swallow that. You'd better go. Or we'll part in anger.

Pause.

MELANIE. That's very sensible. I agree with that. *(She turns to go, stops.)* One other thing.

Pause.

YOUNG GOCHER. What?

MELANIE. Do you still fancy me?

YOUNG GOCHER. You need to know that, do you?

MELANIE. I'd like to. Out of interest.

Pause.

YOUNG GOCHER. No.
MELANIE. Liar.

She goes out. GOCHER *deliberately turns away, avoids watching her.*

YOUNG GOCHER. Finish with women! Finish with 'em! Easier said than done, of course, but possible. Has been done. Men have done it. Men with purpose. Men with work. *(Pause.)* Had more than my share. More squirming tarts than I could get my fingers up. As the Yodelling Tramp. Sliming up the dressing-room. Done everything. All that was possible. All that presented itself to the imagination of a normal man. *(Pause.)* Just party work now. Like minds in the party. Not likely to damage you. The real intimacy of solidarity. *(Pause, then suddenly his face creases.)* MELANIE!

Blackout.

Scene Fifteen

A second-class compartment of the Brighton train. A train seat, along which GOCHER *is lying. By the window,* LEARY, *looking out. Sound of train movement.*

LEARY. The Trans-Europ Express. The Arctic Circle via East Croydon, Redhill, Haywards Heath. *(He looks to* GOCHER.) Good time. Making good time, aren't we?
GOCHER. The air tastes better. The air that struggling men have breathed.
LEARY *(taking deep lungfuls).* Typical Poland! Get a lungful, grandad.
GOCHER. How does it feel to be free, son? Does it ache?
LEARY. Novel. Very novel, I admit.
GOCHER *(contemplating him).* The screw who turned. The cossack who would not wield the knout . . . *(Pause.)* If they'd caught us, they would have had you certified.
LEARY. Maybe I needed it.
GOCHER. The Englishman! A decent motive is a weakness in his eyes.
LEARY. Don't knock England. I don't want it knocked.
GOCHER. It was where I was bled white, Leary. It was the scene of my living death.
LEARY. My father was Irish. By descent. He hated England. He said he had never hated any place so much. But then he had never been anywhere else either. He was born in Clapham, he lived in Clapham, and he died there. So his opinion wasn't worth that much.
GOCHER. Don't give into patriotism, Leary. It's their way of closing yer eyes . . . (LEARY *looks at him. Long pause.)* You are sitting on the Trans-Europ Express, and I don't think you know why. You have done an

action out of impulse, and it's frightened you. *(Pause.)* Pity's not enough.
You've got to find an ideology.

They look at one another. LEARY *suddenly points out of the window.*

LEARY.   Look! It's the USSR!
GOCHER.   We never stopped in Poland! What happened to Poland?
LEARY.   No one wanted to get off.
GOCHER *(grabbing the bottled hand).*   Tovarish! Your homeland!
LEARY.   Congratulations, Tov!
GOCHER.   His long exile, over!
LEARY *(breathing deep).*   Soviet air!
GOCHER.   'Arise, ye starvlings from your slum—bers, Arise, ye crim—i—
nals of want!' (*He breaks down into a fit of deep coughing.* LEARY
watches, helplessly. Pause. GOCHER *recovers.*) We'll have trouble
finding him. (LEARY *looks appalled.*) A skeleton with one hand missing.
Won't be easy. *(Pause.)* Will it? Not easy.
LEARY.   Can't you remember the spot? You dug the grave.
GOCHER.   I dug it.
LEARY.   Well, then . . .
GOCHER.   They don't mark graves. Not in the middle of a civil war, eh,
Tovarish? Not when you are manure. No green chips and alabaster. Just
slap, face down in yer overcoat.
LEARY.   Not marked . . .
GOCHER.   Turn 'em all up! Turn up all the graves, Leary!
LEARY.   Why not? Might as well while we're about it . . .
GOCHER.   Then plough me in. I should not be here. In a proper society I
would have been shot years ago. I've outlasted myself, haven't I? I am a
fucking specimen.

Pause, then on the spur of the moment, LEARY *jumps up and pulls the
communication cord. The train's brakes screech agonizingly.*

LEARY.   I saw it! Murmansk in the distance! I saw it! Come on, jump out!

The train has stopped, GOCHER *wearily picks himself off the seat, moves to
the door, stops.*

GOCHER.   Christ, Leary, when I was here last . . .
LEARY.   Don't hang about . . .
GOCHER.   My life has been a dry shout . . . (LEARY *looks at him.*) I am
full of pity for myself. (*He begins to weep.* LEARY *is embarrassed,
uncertain what to do.*)
LEARY.   Get down!

Blackout.

Scene Sixteen

*A burning whisky warehouse in the London Docks during an air raid, 1942.
In the blackout, a furious blowing of whistles. Red lights rise to show*
YOUNG GOCHER, *an auxiliary fireman, feeling his way along the back
wall of the theatre, clasping and following a white tape. He has a whistle in his
mouth, which he blows in response to whistles off. The tape he is following
suddenly stops. He holds the limp, broken end in his hand, immobilized. The
whistles die out. Then he begins tracing it back the other way, whistling
urgently. After some yards, the tape ends again. For some seconds he stares
at the broken end. Then he takes the whistle out of his mouth.*

GOCHER *(horrified)*. H—E—L—P! Don't panic. Mustn't panic.
Remember drill. Drill... drill... drill... FUCKING DRILL! Sit down.
Sit down. Think drill. *(He sits.)* Now drill... yes... drill... *(He thinks
desperately, then, suddenly.)* Do not swallow hot air! Got one! *(He goes
blank again.)* This is a whisky fire. Special notes for whisky fires. Last
week's lecture... *(Suddenly, with horror.)* I don't know which floor I'm
on!

*He falls forward in a fit of despair, head between his knees. As he sits there,
sound of a crate of bottles being dragged along, which precedes the entrance
of* STAVELEY, *drunk and wearing a party hat. He is partially engulfed by
coloured streamers and is following the same tape that* GOCHER *followed.
He too stops when the tape does, looks at it, slow of comprehension.*

STAVELEY. Shit. *(Pause.)* Shitty shit. *(He takes a pull at the whisky
bottle in his hand, but finding it empty, tosses it aside and takes another
out of the crate. He then sits on the crate and starts undoing it.)* Going to
die now. Bugger it. Going to sodding well die. *(He takes a long drink.)*
Cynthia says... this tart says... got to get more liquor... party's going off
the boil... but all the off-licences are shut... bloody blitz has shut the off-
licences... well, collect it from your warehouse, she says... in the car... so
through this sodding blitz... this particularly awful sodding blitz... with
one hand up her knickers and the other on the steering wheel... with
coppers shouting at us... we drive into this dockland dump... this
particularly loathsome dockland dump to get this whisky... and spent
hours with the watchman telling him it is my whisky... my OWN whisky
he is guarding or pretending to... and his fucking alsatian with its nose up
her... MY OWN alsation, technically... and she says... Cynthia says
never had it in a warehouse... would I like to... up against the crates...
and hardly got her going when the fucking interfering dog appears...
which frightens her... she kicks the bottle over, smashes it... I drop my
fag-end and WHOOSH... up she goes... the ground floor and the effing
alsatian... Cynthia... the watchman, Loch Glengarry, everything... I
ran upwards... the only way...
GOCHER. You what?
STAVELEY. Ran upwards.
GOCHER. DROPPED YOUR FAG!

STAVELEY.   One hand . . . you see . . . down the knickers . . . and the other—
GOCHER.   They called us out!
STAVELEY.   Firemen . . .
YOUNG GOCHER.   We were called out!
STAVELEY.   Would have been, yes . . . direct line to the station.
YOUNG GOCHER.   Thought it was a bomb. Thought it was because of bombing!
STAVELEY.   Might well have been, could well have been a bomb. Very likely bomb would have got it if Cynthia—or rather, alsatian hadn't got there first.

Pause. YOUNG GOCHER *looks at him.*

YOUNG GOCHER.   I know you. You are Staveley.
STAVELEY.   The blenders, yes. Loch Glengarry. You must have seen the bottles. *(He holds a bottle up.)* This lake thing on the label . . . is a loch . . . you see . . . it's Scottish . . . for lake . . . the waters of which contain . . . I don't exactly know what they contain, I haven't been there . . . but the distillery came up and I . . . I have a weakness for the label and I—
GOCHER.   FUCK!
STAVELEY.   Wrong, of course, in retrospect . . . seeing where it's led me to . . .
YOUNG GOCHER.   And ME.
STAVELEY.   Both of us.
YOUNG GOCHER.   And others.
STAVELEY.   The dog, you mean.
YOUNG GOCHER.   Not the sodding dog! Firemen!
STAVELEY.   Oh yes, absolutely.
YOUNG GOCHER.   I don't want to die for your bloody whisky!
STAVELEY.   Understandable.
YOUNG GOCHER.   You have murdered me!
STAVELEY.   No . . .
YOUNG GOCHER.   Yes, MURDERED me!
STAVELEY.   No . . . no . . . listen . . .
YOUNG GOCHER.   This is your fire! Do you admit this is your fire?
STAVELEY.   No.
YOUNG GOCHER.   Christ!
STAVELEY.   It's England's fire. You chaps are putting out England's fires.
YOUNG GOCHER.   This is your property. So it's your fire.
STAVELEY.   Listen. Listen.
YOUNG GOCHER.   Jesus Christ . . . !
STAVELEY.   Explain. Explain. *(He waves his arm in an arc.)* All this . . . all this dockland . . . is insured. I am insured. So frankly . . . not wanting to hurt your feelings but . . . personally . . . don't give a bugger if you chaps turn up or not. If Hitler bombs it, well, good luck. Frankly, happy with the insurance . . . see?

YOUNG GOCHER *is staring at him.*

YOUNG GOCHER.   Hundreds of blokes have died in these docks . . .

STAVELEY.   Regret that. Sincerely regret that, obviously.

YOUNG GOCHER.   Liar.

STAVELEY.   They still died for England because—

YOUNG GOCHER.   Died for you!

STAVELEY.   For England because if you listen . . . insurance people have got to pay . . . pay me, that is . . . and if too many . . . pay outs . . . too many burnt out warehouses . . . what happens? Premiums go up, you see. Premiums. Know premiums? And that means everybody has to fork out more . . . dip into their pockets, see? Hits everyone. Little men with families. Car insurance. Are you with me? (GOCHER *is silent.* STAVELEY *takes a pull at the bottle. Pause.*) I used to be in music. Not playing. Before that, in the army. What about you?

YOUNG GOCHER.   Used to be in music. Before that, in the army.

STAVELEY.   Where?

YOUNG GOCHER.   Murmansk.

STAVELEY.   Know it. Well . . . know the barracks. *(He takes more whisky.)*

YOUNG GOCHER.   Give us the bottle.

STAVELEY *(he gives* GOCHER *a new bottle from the crate).*   Help yourself, old chap.

YOUNG GOCHER.   If you're going to die, best be drunk.

STAVELEY.   Isn't it the fumes will kill us? Rather than fire? I didn't really want to roast. Flame to flesh, I mean. Prefer a stupor.

YOUNG GOCHER.   That's the staircase going . . .

STAVELEY.   Rather die with a man. Funny that. Not homo or anything. Not even at school. But when it comes to dying, prefer it with a man.

YOUNG GOCHER.   Well, you just had a woman, didn't you?

STAVELEY.   Cynthia?

YOUNG GOCHER.   Whatever her name was.

STAVELEY.   I think it was Cynthia.

YOUNG GOCHER.   If she was here now . . . I would have her . . .

STAVELEY.   You could have her.

YOUNG GOCHER.   Even after you had been there.

STAVELEY.   Get your mind off—*(He takes a pull at the bottle.)* I AM SCARED! (*He looks at* GOCHER, *gritting his teeth, gets up, and moves to sit next to him.*) I am not a homo, but must say about women, have never felt complete DESIRE. I mean, in the fullest sense of thinking—WHAT WAS THAT?

YOUNG GOCHER.   Ceiling.

STAVELEY.   Ceiling?

YOUNG GOCHER.   Coming down.

STAVELEY *(less drunk, but more nervous).*   Of thinking that the body of the woman was—wondrous. Pure. And that going in her body I was—Christ—WHAT WAS THAT—

YOUNG GOCHER.   Timbers. Falling timbers.

STAVELEY.   Sharing in an act of—purity. (*He is shakin.* GOCHER *puts his arm round him.*) It should be pure, shouldn't it? It should be that—

There is a sudden cacophony of whistles. GOCHER *leaps to his feet, finds his own whistle, blows desperately. More whistles respond.*

YOUNG GOCHER. Coming, mate!
STAVELEY. What's that? Are we—
YOUNG GOCHER. No. Not you, Staveley.
STAVELEY *(joyous).* Way out, is there?
YOUNG GOCHER. No. No more Staveleys in the world.

STAVELEY *looks at him, dimly. The whistles blow frantically.* GOCHER *grabs the axe from his belt and raises it. Blackout.*

Scene Seventeen

Somewhere on the South Downs, as indicated by a National Trust sign-post or a litter notice. Some gulls or general bird song. LEARY *enters supporting* GOCHER. *He is carrying the bottle.*

GOCHER. Oi, Russians! Get an eyeful! The hideous spectacle of a man who tried to chuck a spanner in the works! In this land of heroes, a dead man looking for a dead man, a wet fart blown down the bumhole of the world . . . *(Pause.* LEARY *sits disconsolately on the ground.)* Russians! *(He looks around.)* Where are they? The Muzhiks and the Proletariat?
LEARY. At work.
GOCHER. They would work. They have something to work for. I worked once. I was in sewerage.
LEARY. You never said.
GOCHER. In POLITICS, wasn't I? What have I been telling you, I was in POLITICS!
LEARY. All right, all right . . .
GOCHER. Christ, what did I tell you, how to tell a man in England he can change the world only produces terror in his bowels! *(Pause.)* You work in politics, you are in sewerage . . .
LEARY *(Pause. Pointing off stage).* Murmansk. In the distance . . .
GOCHER *(screwing up his eyes).* Yeah . . . it was something like that . . .
LEARY. Bound to have changed. With progress.

Pause. GOCHER *suddenly turns on him.*

GOCHER. No snow! NO SODDING SNOW!
LEARY *(groping).* In summer?
GOCHER *(hesitates, uncertain).* Always, I thought. Always . . .
LEARY. How old were you?
GOCHER. I was a kid . . .

Pause. LEARY *looks at* GOCHER, *who gazes at the ground.*

LEARY. 'Snow was fall—ing, snow on snow, sno—o—ow on snow, In the bleak mid-winter, lo—o—ong ago . . .' *(Pause.)* Anyway, the ice-cap's melting. So I read. We are swapping climates with the blacks. They've got our rain. They'll do very well now, you watch.

GOCHER.   Come on. Tovarish is waiting.

LEARY.   We will be a desert. Smelly goatskins will be treasures.

GOCHER.   Dig, will yer, Leary? For Christ's sake, dig!

LEARY.   No hurry, is there? No desperate hurry. He has waited fifty years, another ten minutes isn't going to—

GOCHER.   I'm dying. I am dying . . . can't yer see that, son?

LEARY *(looks at him a few moments)*. Right. *(Pause.)* All right.

They begin scraping at the earth, on their hands and knees, moving slowly round the stage, GOCHER *rests almost at once. He looks at the bottle.*

GOCHER.   It's a better hand than mine now . . . funny how the nails kept growing . . .

LEARY.   Like a Chinese mandarin.

GOCHER.   When they were all busted with hard labour . . . to end up like a manicured Chinese ponce . . .

LEARY.   BUGGER! Broke me pen knife. BUGGER IT!

GOCHER *(settling back wearily)*. We aren't gonna make it, Leary . . .

LEARY.   Give it time. Lot of ground here.

GOCHER.   We're not. We're not . . .

LEARY *(feigning discovery)*. What's this! What's this!

GOCHER.   I used to think, when you came to the Day of Judgement, if there was one, and the angel said, what did you do? It would be all right to say, I tried. I did try. I fucking tried! But now I know if I was the angel, I'd say, bugger off then, if all you ever did was try. We have no room for triers, only succeeders walking about the heavenly grass, listening to the heavenly top ten. All the miserable triers, all the good school-kids bent over their desks, the angel would just boot 'em. The world isn't dented by the soft slippers of the triers, only by the boots of the doers . . .

LEARY.   Did you see this? What's this?

GOCHER *(casually turns his head)*.   A bone.

LEARY *(glowing)*.   Yeah. A bone. (*He gazes at* GOCHER *with a fanatical expression.*)

GOCHER.   All right, a bone.

LEARY.   A BONE.

Pause. GOCHER *stares at* LEARY, *fathoming. Long moment of tension.*

GOCHER.   WHAT ARE YOU TRYING TO DO TO ME!

Pause. LEARY *is deflated.*

LEARY.   I'm saying that—I'm saying—

GOCHER.   WHAT'S YOUR GAME, LEARY? (LEARY *shrugs, drops the bone on the ground.*) Could be ANY bone. Russia's choc a bloc with bones. Why THAT bone?

Pause.

LEARY *(back in business)*.   I wasn't saying it's THE bone. I never said that, did I? I'm saying it's encouraging to have even found a bone. I agree, it's probably not Tovarish's. Chances are against it, I expect . . .

GOCHER *continues to stare at him resentfully, then at last he turns and starts scraping at the ground. LEARY watches him for some seconds, resting on his knees. Then he turns away and continues digging. Suddenly GOCHER lets out a cry.*

GOCHER.   FOUND IT!

LEARY *turns to see GOCHER holding up to the sky the same small piece of animal bone he had tossed away. Long pause.*

LEARY.   Ah . . . *(Pause.)* Ah, well . . .

Blackout.

Scene Eighteen

YOUNG GOCHER *in a spot, holding a baby in a shawl.*

YOUNG GOCHER.   Come to Platform 17, she says, at Swindon Central. I have something for you. So I went. To my Mrs, who had not written for six months, who had not given me an address, who could have been dead for all I know. And there she gives it to me. The baby. By the bookstall with a troop-train full of airmen looking on. And not one word. Deliberately not one word. Nor me neither. Not one word. *(Pause.)* And when I get back on the London train, there is this little ticket pinned to her, stuck to her shawl. Elizabeth. After the queen, no doubt. Which I chucked out the window, and when we got to Paddington, went direct to a comrade who had been expelled from Oxford. I want to name my daughter in a fashion appropriate, I said, to the historic condition. And we agreed, that after the war there will be communism in these islands because our soldiers are not just going to hand their rifles back. Not like before. Oh, no, we are the masters now. So he suggested the name Fate. In Greek. Which is Moira. Which I liked the sound of anyway. *(Pause.)* As for her mother, I heard nothing.

The spot flicks out.

Scene Nineteen

LEARY *is looking at GOCHER, who holds the bone fragment.*

LEARY.   Collar, is it? Collar bone?
GOCHER *(categorically).*   Wrist.
LEARY.   Wrist bone. *(He picks up the bottled hand. Examines it from underneath.)* Perfect fit . . . *(He looks at GOCHER. Pause.)*
GOCHER.   Inter them, then. We have found the resting place of Tovarish. (LEARY *looks sceptically at GOCHER, who reveals nothing. LEARY kneels and starts to scrape a hole. After a few seconds an old man appears, in a grey flannel suit, wearing thick lensed spectacles. He is holding outstretched an envelope. He stops, the arm rigid. Pause.)* He wants to give

yer something. (LEARY *looks doubtful.*) Take it, then. (LEARY *gets up, takes the envelope from the man, opens it. Pause.*) What is it?

LEARY *(unconvincingly).*   It's in Russian . . .

Pause.

GOCHER.   I can read Russian.

Their eyes meet. LEARY *gives the card to* GOCHER.

GOCHER.   It says 'The Holder of this card is an inmate of the Eastbourne Hospital.' (LEARY *looks uneasily at him.*) There is a number you can ring. *(Pause.)* Should ring. *(Pause.)* Must ring.

LEARY.   No telephone, that I can see.

GOCHER.   No roubles, either.

LEARY.   Yeah, well, that's another thing . . .

Pause. Suddenly the old man begins to jerk his head convulsively.

STAVELEY.   G—G—G—G—G

LEARY.   I don't think we can have this. In the middle of a funeral.

STAVELEY.   G—G—G—G—

LEARY.   He's dribbling. Jesus Christ. It spoils the dignity of the occasion. What's he doing here in any case? In the middle of the— *(He stops, looking for the right word.)*

GOCHER *(helping him).*   Steppe.

STAVELEY.   GYS—O—MIN. *(He raises two fingers. Pause.)*

GOCHER.   On a coach trip. With a lot of other loonies. Got left behind . . .

STAVELEY.   D—D—D—D—

LEARY.   Bloody hell . . .

STAVELEY.   D—D—D—D—

LEARY.   I don't like illness. I am sorry but I can't stick illnesses!

STAVELEY.   DUR—A—BIL. *(He raises three fingers of the other hand.)*

LEARY.   Got to shift him, haven't we? *(He makes a move towards* STAVELEY).

STAVELEY.   STA—VE—LEY. *(He throws back his head, mouth open for the reception of pills.* LEARY *freezes in his tracks.* STAVELEY *remains in this posture, hands raised, head back.)*

GOCHER.   Look at his head. Is there a scar on the back of his head?

LEARY *(gingerly examines* STAVELEY's *pate).*   Several. And a little bit of silver plate . . .

GOCHER *looks at* LEARY, *moves slowly across and grinds the bone fragment with his foot.* LEARY *looks anxious.*

GOCHER.   Tovarish was no bloody sheep . . .

Blackout.

Scene Twenty

A bedsitting room, Croydon, 1952. Two chairs. In one, YOUNG GOCHER, *now 50. In the other,* MOIRA, *aged 7.*

YOUNG GOCHER.   Our home. Croydon, 1952. *(Pause.)* Darling. Listen, darling. Explain to you. Darling sit still, daddy explain to you. What daddy gets so wild about, which upsets darling, naturally. See daddy like that, horrible. So are you listening? Calmly explain, then. *(Pause.)* No, you are not listening! Are you? What did I say? *(Pause.)* No, well, I didn't. So listen, please. MOIRA! *(pause.)* Because how nice if everybody was nice all the time. If we were all nice, If it was a nice place, in fact. People are always telling us what a nice place it is. But what a fib that is. What a whopper! We look around, we use our eyes, and is it nice? No, it is not nice. It is quite horrible.

      MOIRA!   *(Pause.)*   The word for that is REALITY. RE—AL—ITY. The actual thing. The REAL thing. The thing we keep on bumping into, and which is neve really very nice, which is awful, in fact. Despite those whoppers they tell us, we see it and it isn't nice. *(Pause.)* Please don't get down. No, not yet. I haven't finished yet. Look, this is for your benefit! *(Pause.)* So we ask questions, don't we? Because we are humans, and humans will ask questions. You can't stop 'em. It is a human thing. And the reason we ask questions is, we have this sense of what should be. Goodness know where that comes from. Anywhere. Out of the sky, maybe. We just has this funny sense. And that is called JUSTICE. You have heard that word, I'm sure. I have used that word a lot. I am always using it. A funny word. I don't know its origin. MOIRA! *(He closes his eyes.)* DO NOT MOVE. When I'm talking DO NOT MOVE. *(He opens his eyes.)* Good girl. Good girl. *(Pause.)* Justice, you see. It cries out. It is always crying out. You look around you, and before you know where you are, it's crying out. We ask for nice, not nasty. And nothing could be easier, you might think. You like niceness, don't you? So do I. But some people, they don't like niceness, or to be more accurate, they want the niceness for themselves. They want to HOG THE NICENESS. *(Pause.)* So we have go grab it. We have to drag it out their hands, and then what do they do? They attack us! Yes, they set about us! Violently! They attack us, they set on us the WHOLE FORCE OF THE BOURGEOIS STATE! THEY PUT THE STATE AGAINST THE PEOPLE! LOOK WHAT THEY HAVE DONE TO ME BECAUSE I WOULD NOT PLAY THE BANJO TO THEIR BLOODY LIES! A FATHER AND A CHILD IN THIS DISGUSTING ROOM! LOOK AT THE FILTH THEY FLING US IN, THE BASTARDS, THE PARASITIC BASTARDS, THEY DRINK OUR BLOOD! I WILL KILL THEM, I WILL KILL THEIR BABIES, IT WILL BE A SLAUGHTER WHEN WE'VE FINISHED, A FAIR BLOODY SLAUGHTER, LET ME, GOD! *(He bursts into a fit of weeping, rocking back and forwards in his chair, hands to his face.)* Daddy upset darling . . . sorry, darling . . . sorry, sorry, sorry, love . . .

Lights fade to black.

Scene Twenty-One

On the Downs, some time later. Darkness is falling. STAVELEY *is standing, hands by his sides.* GOCHER *is sitting on the ground.* LEARY *is standing behind* STAVELEY.

LEARY.   Do you understand the charges? *(Pause.)* I will ask you again. Do you understand the charges? *(Pause.)* STAVELEY! YOU DOG! *(Pause.)* All right, all right, all right. You are here on a charge of being an enemy of the people. Do you plead guilty or not guilty?

STAVELEY.   G—G—G—G—

LEARY.   Guilty. Thank you.

STAVELEY.   GYS—O—MIN.

LEARY.   There is no Gysomin. Will you shut up about Gysomin. Call the worker Gocher.

GOCHER.   He has got to have his tablets. It says on the card he has got to—

LEARY *(as if in court)*.   GOCHER!

GOCHER.   GOCHER!

LEARY.   GOCHER! *(Pause.)* Comrade Gocher, take the remains of Tovarish in your right hand and repeat after me. I swear—

GOCHER *(holding the bottle)*.   I swear . . .

LEARY.   That the evidence I shall give—

GOCHER.   That the evidence I shall give . . .

LEARY.   Shall be for the people, for all the peole, and for nobody but the people, so help me Tovarish.

GOCHER.   I swear.

LEARY.   Worker Gocher, do you recognise the accused?

GOCHER.   He is a capitalist.

LEARY.   He is a capitalist. Thank you.

GOCHER.   He was a capitalist. Sorry.

LEARY.   Once a capitalist, always a capitalist, surely Comrade?

GOCHER.   He is retired.

LEARY.   All capitalists are retired. By definition.

GOCHER.   I mean he is—

LEARY.   I know what you mean, Comrade. You mean he is no longer an active parasite, he is a passive one.

GOCHER.   I mean I don't believe—

LEARY.   Call Leary.

GOCHER.   LEARY!

LEARY.   LEARY!

GOCHER.   LEARY!

LEARY *(taking the bottle)*.   I swear. *(He puts it down.)* Comrade Leary, what is your profession? I am a prison warder. Comrade Leary, what can you tell us about the accused?

STAVELEY.   D—D—D—D—
LEARY.   SHUDDUP!
STAVELEY.   D—D—D—D—
LEARY *(yelling in his face).*   Will you shut up! (STAVELEY *goes silent.*
LEARY *closes his eyes in irritation.)*
STAVELEY.   DUR—A—BIL. *(He tosses back his head.)*
LEARY.   Lost me—fuck—fuck— *(He recollects.)* I have a scar. Will you
witness my scar?
GOCHER.   SCAR! SCAR!
LEARY *(rolling up his sleeve to show a wound).*   My stabbed flesh, my
gashed vein, spurting on filthy corridors. This scar, whose lips were not so
long ago wide open yelling, this scar was earned by me in the act of
restraining a man who had a longing to live in the world and who believed
the bars would listen to him. This scar I took for keeping a man down, a
man who was a murderer, a torturer, a thief, a disgusting and degrading
specimen. For ten years I worked in a screaming menagerie of greedy men,
who had been trapped and howled in there and ripped their keepers with
secretly manufactured knives, sharpened on the whetstones of their prison
walls. And that murderer who maimed me as I stood between him and the
treasures of your drawing room, the little that he learned in life, he learned
from you. You made him, and having made him, put my stupid body in
between, so every time they slung their piss buckets and beat their doors
until my head burst with the noise, it was the music of your system in my
ears! I accuse you, in the name of all our dead and dying criminals, on
behalf of every prisoner and screw, through all the useless scuffles of their
years, I accuse you and demand the highest penalty!

Pause.

GOCHER.   Good, son. Very good.

Pause, LEARY *rolls down his sleeve.*

LEARY.   The people find him guilty.
GOCHER.   Got to. After a speech like that.

Pause.

LEARY.   Do you want to do it, or shall I?
GOCHER.   What?
LEARY.   It.

Pause.

GOCHER.   Don't follow yer.
LEARY.   The penalty.
GOCHER.   What penalty?
LEARY.   He has been tried and found guilty. So who is the People's
executioner? (GOCHER *chuckles.)* Grandad . . . ? Who's DOING him?
(GOCHER *just stares.)* All right, I will. Find us a brick.
GOCHER.   Christ . . .
LEARY.   Flint Rock. Anything . . . *(He looks around.)*

GOCHER.   You're not killing him . . . ?

LEARY.   Tovarish says to know your enemy.

GOCHER.   Yeah, but he's a—

LEARY.   Look, is Staveley your enemy or not? Is he a man who has killed workers? Is he a murdering capitalist or not?

GOCHER.   He may have done—

LEARY.   Well, then, do not spit on Tovarish. *(He carries on looking for a brick.)*

GOCHER.   He is an old geezer. He is mental, Leary, show a bit of—

LEARY.   No pity and no tolerance! I say that, to this country which has pissed and dribbled with its tolerance. We vomit up all tolerance. The workers' state is not tolerant!

GOCHER.   But he is—you can see what he is—

LEARY *(coming to him).* Look, ask Tovarish. Tovarish will tell you there can be no tolerance. You tolerate only what cannot hurt you.

GOCHER.   He can't hurt you.

LEARY.   How do we know?

GOCHER.   He is mental, you can see. He has wandered off a coach trip. He is barmy, Leary!

LEARY.   Trickery.

GOCHER.   Christ . . .

LEARY.   Short memory you have, grandad. All of a sudden he is a sweet and gentle OAP.

GOCHER.   There is nothing in his head, Leary.

LEARY.   There is guilt in his head. You told me! (GOCHER *is silent.* LEARY *looks at him with contempt.)* You cannot serve the people if you cannot pull the trigger. If there had been a revolution here, you would have crept away with wet eyes to your family . . .

GOCHER.   Give me Tov.

LEARY.   No.

GOCHER.   Give it to me.

LEARY.   You are not fit to have Tov.

GOCHER.   Christ, do not lose sight of your humanity! You have so much good in you!

LEARY.   To be licked up by that specimen. To be sucked on by his class.

GOCHER.   Keep an open heart, son. Feed your heart. The angrier you feel, the more you have to feed the heart!

LEARY.   I do what Tov says!

GOCHER.   Fuck him! He was an ordinary bloke, that's all. Think for yourself. They stuck Lenin under glass, and look what they have done in his name.

LEARY.   To hear you say that . . . you burn me . . . you sod . . .

GOCHER.   Criticize. Always criticize.

LEARY.   Revise, you mean.

GOCHER.   I mean—

LEARY.   REVISE!

Pause. GOCHER *looks at him.*

GOCHER. Bust the bottle, Leary. Bust it. (LEARY *shakes his head.*) It's mine.

LEARY. Tov belongs to the people. No one can own Tovarish.

Suddenly, with a supreme effort, GOCHER lurches towards the hand. LEARY sweeps it away. GOCHER falls with a groan. At that moment, heavenly lighting floods the stage. Backed by a choir. The sound of a man singing the negro spiritual 'Gospel Train' is heard off stage, growing louder. TOVARISH enters, shunting round the stage in his classic engine mime. He is wearing his driver's outfit, but in a heavenly transformation, and holds a bunch of dahlias in one hand. The other sleeve is empty.

TOVARISH.   This train—bound for Hea—ven—this train,
This train—bound for Hea—ven—this train,
All God's chillun got arms and legs,
This train—bound for Hea—ven—this train.

GOCHER (*struggles onto his elbows, gazing around in terminal delight*). On my way, Tovarish! Get shot of the mortal coils, mate!

TOVARISH.   All souls speak Russian, comrade!

GOCHER.   I'll be buggered . . .

TOVARISH.   Smirnoff! Dubrovnik! Moskavitch!

GOCHER.   I am floating! I am floating out of it!

He sinks back slowly, dies as TOVARISH completes a final circuit. He goes out. The choir recedes. LEARY looks at GOCHER a moment then lays his hands across his chest. As he is doing this, sound of voices calling off.

SEARCH PARTY.   Stave—ley! Stave—ley!

Occasional torch flashes illumine the stage. LEARY picks up the bottled hand and starts to hurry away. He stops, goes back to STAVELEY, who is perfectly immobile, as before. He looks at him for some seconds.

LEARY.   Not mad. Deceitful bastard NOT MAD!

Pause. Sound of search party calling STAVELEY's name. LEARY goes off. Pause. Slowly, STAVELEY emerges from his immobility, his face develops a guilty, schoolboyish expression, conspiratorial, insane.

STAVELEY.   Got—the—Pic—asso—Got—the—Pic—asso— (*He carefully takes a tattered, cheap reproduction of a celebrated Picasso from his jacket pocket, and gazes at it gloatingly, looking guiltily from side to side.*) Got—the—Pic—asso—Got—the—Pic—asso—

The lights fade to black.